EUROPEAN AIR LAW ASSOCIATION CONFERENCE PAPERS

11

EUROPEAN AIR LAW ASSOCIATION
CONFERENCE PAPERS

11

AIRLINE LIABILITY

A seminar on liability and claims handling in the airline
and aerospace industries

Munich, 12 May 1997

edited by
P.D. Dagtoglou and P.N. Ehlers

ANT.N. SAKKOULAS PUBLISHERS
Athens
KLUWER LAW INTERNATIONAL
The Hague • London • Boston

Distribution in the U.S.A. and Canada
Kluwer Law International
675, Massachusetts Avenue
Cambridge, MA 02139/USA

Distribution in all other countries except Greece
Kluwer Law International
Distribution Centre
P.O. Box 322
3300 AH Dordrecht, The Netherlands

ISBN 960-232-721-9 (Sakkoulas)
ISBN 90-411-0542-5 (Kluwer)

Ant. N. Sakkoulas Publishers
69, Solonos Street
106 79 Athens, Greece
tel. +(30 1) 3618198, +(30 1) 3615440

Kluwer Law International
P.O. Box 85889
2508 CN The Hague, The Netherlands
tel. + (31 70) 3081500

Email: info@ant-sakkoulas.gr
Url: www.ant-sakkoulas.gr

Printed and bound by Antony Rowe Ltd, Eastbourne

Contents

8

Opening Address by Professor P.D. Dagtoglou

President of the European Air Law Association, London/Athens

I have great pleasure in opening the Liability Seminar of the European Air Law Association in Munich. The Association has not been in the Bavarian capital before and we are delighted to come at least as near to it as its thriving airport. Some of us have, I understand, used the opportunity of the seminar to spend a weekent in this pleasant city.

This seminar would not have taken place but for the initiative and the untiring efforts of Dr. Nikolai Ehlers, of Ehlers and Partner, Munich. I am sure that I express everyone's wishes if I thank him and his assistants most heartily. I would also like to thank ERC Francona Rückversicherung AG and Flughafen München GmbH for their generous contribution towards the costs of the seminar.

This is the first time EALA ventures on a subject not specifically European. As a matter of fact, history could call the subject of our seminar Japanese. It was after all Japan which first (1982 for domestic and 1992 for international carriers) introduced unlimited liability for passenger injury or death.

Japan's initative was, it seems, prompted to a great extent by its courts which, finding the limits of the Warsaw Convention unacceptably low and inequitably rigid, resulted in the acceptance of criminal responsibility for considerable numbers of airline (but also Ministry of Transport and aircraft manufacturer) officials who were somehow, in the framework of their duties, connected with the accident. In Japanese legal thought and tradition, the lower the civil liablity the higher the criminal responsibility. In the words of Professor Sekiguchi of Komazawa University, Tokyo, there is a Japanese custom "that tends to link criminal responsibility with civil fault and the degree of compensation awarded has severe repercussions on the generally accepted principles of criminal responsibility" (Masao Sekigushi, Why Japan was compelled to opt for unlimited liability, Annals of Air and Space Law 1995, 337 et seq., 348).

This seems to have concentrated wonderfully the minds of all concerned. If unlimited liability would normally preclude criminal responsibility, unlimited liability had to be introduced. This after all meant in practice no more than bringing air carrier liability in line with automobile liability. Moreover, introducing unlimited liability was probably also a marketing strategy demonstrating to passengers worldwide the Japanese airlines' confidence in their safety record.

Since the "Japanese initiative" there have been several others, especially by ICAO, IATA, ECAC and EU, although none of them has a yet been completed.

In Europe however, and for reasons ranging from fairness towards passengers to the image of air transport, there seems to be a general consensus on the desirability of unlimited liability in case of death or injury of a passenger. The European Union issued already in 1992 a consultation paper on passenger liability in aircraft accidents. When in 1995 the IATA Liability Conference in Washington recommended a new enhanced liability package the European Union agreed unconditionally, although the US did so only conditionally. ICAO is at present engaged in a review of the Warsaw Convention and expects to call an intergovernmental conference in the next year. Pending the outcome of this review and intending to enhance it the European Commission proposed in October 1995 a regulation on unlimited passenger liability which would be reviewed as soon as possible after the review of the Warsaw Convention by ICAO. Last February the Council reached a common position on the Commission's proposal. There is no new development on this score as yet, but it is expected that the Transport Council will adopt the new regulation within this year.

*

The Seminar covers every aspect of liability regarding governments and international organisations, carriers and lawyers, manufacturers and airport operators, as well as insurers. Each aspect is scrutinised by panels consisting of outstanding experts from government departments, the European Commission, the ICAO, IATA, airlines, airport operators, insurers and specialist lawyers. We are really delighted that we were able to secure the contribution of so many eminent speakers. We plan to publish in this year all papers in a book to be included as volume no 11 in the series of the European Air Law Association Conference Papers.

We are very pleased that the seminar has attracted participants from not less than eighteen countries and four international organisations.

It is now time for the organiser of this seminar Dr. Nikolai Ehlers to give his introduction and then for the seminar to begin.

The New IATA International Passenger Liability Regime

by Lorne S. Clark

General Counsel and Corporate Secretary
International Air Transport Association (IATA), Geneva

IATA and its Member airlines, which carry over 98% of world-wide scheduled international air traffic, have been embarked upon what can best be termed an historic "rite of passage" from the old *Warsaw Convention limited liability system* initiated in 1929, amended at The Hague in 1955 and supplemented by means of the Montreal (Intercarrier) Agreement of 1966. The new *IATA unspecified limits regime*, founded on the special contract provision of the Convention, stands in bold contrast to the system it supplants.

In particular, the liability provisions governing carriage by air have been irrevocably altered. True, it will take more time to gain the degree of universal acceptance required to ensure global implementation of the modernised regime. But this is not only inevitable, given the commitment on the part of major carriers around the world, it is also assured by the unyielding determination to provide "unspecified limits" for international passengers on the part of a number of governments.

This audience will be well aware that the international aviation community has been arguing about increasing the Warsaw/Hague limits ever since the ICAO Guatemala City Air Law Conference of 1971 but, unfortunately, without success. Who could ever have imagined that in barely two years since the IATA Airline Liability Conference (ALC) in Washington DC in June 1995, a ground-breaking, modern intercarrier liability regime would be accepted by so many airlines carrying such a high percentage of scheduled international air traffic?

The momentum is gaining and the old order is gone. Against this background IATA is pleased that governments are moving to try to catch up with the airlines by attempting, through ICAO, to develop an entirely new intergovernmental treaty framework for the unspecified limits regime.

It is however important to examine some of the history behind the remarkable developments of 1995-97. On 22 February 1995, the United States Department of Transportation (DOT) issued Immunity Order Number 95-2-44 authorising IATA to conduct intercarrier discussions "to secure the important public benefit of a liability regime that reflects contemporary standards of compensation".

Having much earlier received the requisite "negative clearance" from the European Commission, IATA immediately began a flurry of focused activity and organised the Airline Liability Conference.

The ALC met in Washington in June 1995 and was attended by 67 carriers from around the world, 6 regional airline associations, 3 other industry associations, and representatives of ICAO, the European Commission and the US Departments of Transportation, Justice and State.

The Conference established two Working Groups and mandated the IATA Secretariat to prepare the text of an intercarrier agreement and a "means to secure complete compensation" for international passengers. The eventual intercarrier agreement was to be submitted to the IATA Annual General Meeting (AGM) for approval at the end of October 1995 and then to governments as required.

The two subcommittees fairly quickly developed an "umbrella" Intercarrier Agreement on Passenger Liability (IIA), leaving the particular implementation provisions to be negotiated at the next stage.

The IATA Intercarrier Agreement was then unanimously endorsed by the IATA AGM in Kuala Lumpur, and opened for signature at a symbolic signing ceremony on 31 October 1995. Chief Executive Officers of 12 carriers, representing all of IATATs geographic regions, were the initial signatories. With the impending expiry of DOT Immunity Order 95-2-44 on 31 December 1995, IATA requested and received an extension of immunity to 1 April 1996, later extended to 1 July 1996 to facilitate development of the IIA implementation provisions.

The IIA *umbrella agreement* commits its signatories:

"To take action to waive the limitation of liability on *recoverable compensatory damages* in Article 22 paragraph 1 of the Warsaw Convention as to claims for death, wounding or other bodily injury of a passenger within the meaning of Article 17 of the Convention, so that recoverable compensatory damages be determined and awarded by reference to the law of the domicile of the passenger".

The IATA Secretariat then initiated an intensive effort at the beginning of 1996 to elaborate acceptable provisions to implement the IIA. On 1 February 1996 in Miami, the IATA Legal Working Group approved a draft text of IIA implementing provisions, subject to review with interested governmental authorities. This was followed by high-level meetings with a number of government representatives.

A final meeting of the Legal Working Group was held in Montreal on 3 April 1996. After extensive debate, the Miami text, with minor editorial amendments and now entitled "The Agreement on Measures to Implement the IATA Intercarrier Agreement" (MIA), was unanimously approved. It enshrines the principle of full "recoverable compensatory damages", provides for SDRs 100,000 "strict" liability except where carriers and governments may specifically agree otherwise, retains the *optionality* of domiciliary law for the calculation of damages, does *not* add to the Article 28 fora available to a plaintiff for litigation but does offer carrier signatories other options not inconsistent with the Agreement provided they are in accordance with applicable law.

It is important to underscore, once again, that the Warsaw system has not been "amended" for over three decades, that is since IATA negotiated the 1966 Montreal Agreement (which covers only service to, from, and with an agreed stopping place in, the United States), under the "gun" of the US denunciation of the Warsaw Convention at that time. The 1966 Agreement, of course, did not *amend* the Convention itself, but took advantage of the possibility of the special agreement mechanism to increase passenger liability limits and to voluntarily provide for the waiver of Article 20(1) defences on the part of carriers. The then US Civil Aeronautics Board (CAB) - predecessor of the DOT - later made signature of the Montreal Agreement mandatory for carriers serving the US, failing which they would be "deemed" to be a party in any case. This remains the current situation, although IATA is now working to orchestrate withdrawals from the Agreement, which has effectively been superseded by the IIA/MIA regime.

IATA has long maintained that the Warsaw system is seriously out of date and that the divergent liability limits established around the globe were rooted in the past and did not reflect contemporary community standards in much of today's world. Because of this, the applicable limits of compensation have often been successfully attacked and set aside, by US courts in particular, under the guise of the carrier being guilty of "wilful misconduct", with attendant exposure to unlimited liability under the Warsaw treaty.

Efforts by ICAO and Government representatives in Guatemala City and Montreal, in 1971 and 1975 respectively, to amend the Warsaw system failed. These had been directed to providing for an unbreakable "cap" on airline liability and, in the 1975 Montreal Additional Protocol 3 (MAP 3), to allow for a passenger-funded but government-administered supplemental compensation scheme above and beyond the capped amount, where necessary or desirable (primarily in the US). Barely a year after the Montreal Conference, the proposed "cap" of SDRs 100,000 was already considered inadequate by the US Government - and the amendments to the treaty never came into force for lack of sufficient ratifications, especially the absence of "advice and consent" on the part of the US Senate.

More recently, the 1993-94 attempts by the US Administration to develop a new liability regime under the Warsaw Convention, including the promoting an updated MAP 3, also failed.

IATA Members, reiterating their firm commitment to enhancing the liability benefits to the travelling public, nevertheless must operate within the constraints affecting airlines, which are legally not able to amend international treaties. Since February 1995, they have struggled with the fact that the means of achieving this are far from simple. The Secretariat was thus charged with trying to:

* harmonise the positions of major carriers with that of small and medium-sized airlines, all of them having to put in place appropriate insurance coverage in a relatively short time frame;
* rationalise the needs of carriers already possessing insurance covering "unspecified limits" and those offering only Warsaw, Hague, or other fixed limits, some mandated by governments (with the amounts largely unbeknownst to their passengers);
* preserve the universality of the Warsaw Convention framework, while accommodating inevitable differences in conditions of carriage around the world.

In short, IATA has had to try to overcome all the impediments which have prevented Warsaw reform for the thirty years since the 1966 Montreal Agreement, despite concentrated effort, personal commitment by diligent individuals and, what seemed at various times, a promising environment.

Transcending both the IIA and the MIA, the law of the domicile issue has perhaps given rise to the most comment, often simply because of confusion with the so-called "fifth jurisdiction". Making the "quantum" leap from liability limits often as low as US$ 10,000 (under the unamended Warsaw Convention) to unspecified limits, has undoubtedly posed a serious psychological and financial challenge to many airlines, especially small and medium- sized carriers. In order to *possibly* mitigate their exposure while enshrining the new unspecified limits approach, some carriers prefer an *option* to have the courts calculate the damages according to the law of the passenger's domicile or permanent residence, that is the law most closely connected with the victim.

The MIA spells this out much more clearly and definitively than the IIA "umbrella agreement" i.e. that the law of the domicile is an *option available to the carrier*. Furthermore, many airlines take the position that it would be contrary to and inconsistent with the Warsaw Convention to attempt to create, by intercarrier agreement, a "fifth jurisdiction" - permitting a claimant to litigate in the territory of the passenger's domicile or permanent residence - when this is not a forum available under the Convention. For example the European Commission (if it is in fact within EU competence and if the Member State governments so permit) may impose it on *European Union* carriers and the US authorities may impose it on *their* airlines, but, IATA maintains, neither authority can impose the fifth jurisdiction on third country airlines without amending the Warsaw Convention. In any case, as noted above, the MIA does not purport to add to the jurisdictions set out in the Convention.

The European Commission accepted the IIA and MIA on 26 November 1996. Following a substantive debate between IATA and the US DOT, reflected in the latter's "Show Cause" Order of 3 October 1996, IATATs rejection of the proposed conditions and, finally the DOT's formal approval of the IIA and MIA on 8 January 1997, both intercarrier agreements came into force. For the record and in accordance with its terms, the Director General of IATA declared the MIA "effective" on 14 February 1997.

To date, the IIA has attracted 84 signatories and the MIA has 51 signatures, with both numbers expected to grow in the months ahead.

It cannot be over-emphasised that the old Warsaw/Hague liability world is dead and is being interred. There will be no going back to artificial specified liability limits. The main task for IATA and the international air transport industry in the years ahead will be to try to harmonise as much as possible, within a common framework, the *means* of IIA implementation and, perhaps, to enhance even further the benefits to the travelling public. This will be the central challenge - to ensure the new global approach is just that, *global* in scope, despite possible regional variances to conform to local laws and regulations or the perceived needs of particular environments.

There is a slow but growing recognition of how truly historic the modernisation of the Warsaw system by IATA really is. What ICAO and governments, with the best will in the world, have been unable to do in the more than four decades since the adoption of The Hague Protocol in 1955, the airlines have accomplished, and in less than two years. In the end, this will be to the benefit of the carriers, the passengers, and to the insurers as well.

Governments have now been provided by IATA with a "flight plan" to follow suit. It is up to them to move expeditiously to enshrine the new regime in a binding international legal instrument, a task on which ICAO has just embarked. In this venture it can count on the strong support of IATA and its Member airlines.

However, a word of advice is gratuitously offered: reform Warsaw/Hague as necessary, but *only* as necessary, or risk more "paper" amendments which will lay on the shelf next to the Guatemala City Protocol and Montreal Additional Protocol 3, perhaps providing interesting reading for academics and lawyers but of no benefit whatsoever to the travelling public or the air transport industry!

Liability - The Community Initiative

by F. Sørensen

I am pleased to have been invited to speak about the European perspective on liability limits in the sense of the Warsaw Convention. May I here at the very outset pay tribute to IATA. Without their Kuala Lumpur initiative I doubt that anything fundamental would have happened. Now we see not only air carrier activity but also that governments and ICAO are very active.

I do not need to say very much about the problems with the Warsaw Convention. Everybody agrees that the limits are completely out of touch with any acceptable reality and it is a scandal when an airline still tries to apply these limits. The same is the case of the Montreal Intercarrier agreement.

We started to look into it some years ago and it became very clear in Europe that we had to act. A number of studies were undertaken for the Commission and the results clearly showed the chaos which existed. It was quite impossible for the normal passenger to know whether he was subject to a reasonable liability framework or not. In fact the differences extended not only between international aviation but also between international and domestic. An effort to ensure more transparency would not have sufficed either since the limits were so archaic. Up to date limits would correspond to about 500.000 SDR and the highest applied was only 100.000 SDR. The European Civil Aviation Conference (ECAC) recommended a voluntary increase in limits to 250.000 SDR with an advance payment. The IATA initiative changed the whole situation.

In the European Union we saw the possibility to arrive at a framework which would not depend on voluntary association with the IATA framework but which could be applied to all our air carriers both internationally and domestically. The Commission made a proposal in 1996 and the Council is close to taking a final decision. In fact the decision has been taken in all but the final legal respect. The basic structure is simple. Our air carriers will be subject to strict liablity up to 100.000 SDR. Above 100.000 SDR air carriers may also be liable but they have the possibility to defend themselves. An advance payment is obligatory in case of need. However, in case of death an advance payment of at least 15.000 SDR must be paid. This system is to be applied in case of accidents both internationally and domestically thus ensuring non-discrimination within the air transport market of the Union.

The Commission's proposal has been considered and supported by the European Parliament and a common position has been decided by the Council of Ministers. It is now back at the Parliament for a second reading. However, since most of the Parliament's original amendments have been accepted by the Council few difficulties are expected and a final Council decision is probable in June. Since the legal instrument is a Regulation the new rules will come into effect automatically in all Member States a year later. This delay is motivated by the need for air carriers to reorganise their insurance arrangements.

The Regulation will use the existing framework of the Warsaw Convention. Therefore where strict liability does not exist the principle of presumed liability will exist. This has been maintained, I think, because it was considered as unlikely that a passenger will be able to prove negligence of an air carrier. However, the air carrier will be able to defend itself.

The Regulation also makes it quite clear that air carriers can seek redress from other parties for example the manufacturers if this is where the main responsibility lies. The European system of product liability therefore becomes important. Furthermore, persons who provoke an accident will naturally not be able to claim compensation.

The advance payment which is an integral element of our framework constituted an important part of the ECAC recommendation. It has been taken up in the Regulation. However, instead of defining a minimum or maximum amount it has been decided that it is better to trust that the airlines will be willing to cover real needs of dependants. This may lead to smaller amounts than originally proposed but also to larger ones. The insurance industry in fact pleaded for this system which they said would be more flexible and less bureaucratic. They promised that hardships would be taken care of. Naturally, the situation will be monitored and if difficulties should become apparent I have no doubt that a fixed amount will be reintroduced. Nevertheless in case of death a minimum amount has been fixed because death will nearly always lead to difficult financial situations and the intention is therefore to ensure that these difficulties will be attenuated at least to a certain extent.

In its proposal the Commission also tried to confirm the existence of the internal aviation market of the Union by extending the present jurisdictions to cover not the Member States individually but in case the whole of the Community. This would have been natural since Community air carriers may be active within the whole of the Community. However, this was refused by the Council to a large extent because of US threats in the proposed rulemaking on the IATA agreement.

We would have liked to apply this Regulation also to airlines from third countries. However, it is quite clear that states which have signed the Warsaw Convention cannot oblige third country airlines to apply higher limits than specified in the Convention itself. This very clearly demonstrates the need to modify the Convention. On the other hand it also means that there is a need to ensure that passengers are fully informed about their situation. The Regulation therefore obliges third country airlines, which apply lower standards than prescribed in the Regulation, to inform the passenger at the purchase of the ticket or at the latest at check-in. This is by the way one area where the second reading by the Parliament may lead to a change in the final Regulation. IATA has complained that there is a risk that three different ticket notices might have to be introduced in order to comply with the general Warsaw obligation, the US rules and now the Community rules. This might even be challengeable from a legal point of view. My information is that the Parliament therefore will propose that a) the liability regime will have to be incorporated in the air carrier's conditions of carriage, b) at least this part of the conditions of contract will have to be available at the air carrier's or its agent's counters, and c) that the ticket notice would simply have to say where they can be obtained. In the end, if all air carriers do not limit responsibility then we do not need a ticket notice.

One of the important elements is the question of insurance. It would probably be very costly to try to insure against unlimited liability. The Regulation therefore specifies that a Community Air Carrier must be insured up to at least 100.000 SDR per passenger and thereafter up to a reasonable level. The intention with this element of flexibility is to be able to adjust in accordance with the development in normal payments for damages.

This element became necessary because one of the conditions for a license to a Community air carrier is that the carrier is properly insured.

It is clear that this legislation will have to be taken into account when the discussion takes place on the modification on the Warsaw Convention. However, this will be covered by other speakers. Therefore let me only say that the fact that the European Union has maintained the principle of presumed liability has been an important subject at the discussions in the Legal Committee of ICAO earlier this month since another option in the draft was to put the burden of proof on the passenger. I also believe that the use of the internet has been or will need to be debated unless the jurisdiction which corresponds to the purchase of the ticket will be that one in which the credit card is "swiped". I very much welcome the initiative of ICAO but I am afraid it will not be without difficulties and it may well take considerable time before a sufficient number of states have ratified the amended Convention.

I have tried to describe the legal development in the European Union. It is very close to be definitive. At that time it will have consequences not only within the European Union but also for 12-16 other European countries with which the European Union has association agreements which directly or indirectly commit these countries to harmonise their legislation with the legislation of the European Union. Our initiative must therefore be considered in a larger European framework.

The Down of Unlimited Liability –
What will the Day bring?

by George N. Tompkins, Jr.
Tompkins, Harakas, Elsasser & Tompkins
New York

The era of unlimited liability for passenger injury or death, during the course of international transportation by air within the meaning of the Warsaw Convention, began in 1992 and has envoluted to the point where, in 1997, the international aviation community has found itself facing the dawn of unlimited liability. This has come to pass *without any amendment or replacement* of any of the international agreements generically referred to as the Warsaw system of liability, which emerged in 1929.

Pivotal in this evolutionary process has been the position of the government of the United States of America (USA), as it has sought to expand the rights of USA citizens and residents without risking the collalpse of the Warsaw system or the isolation of the USA from the rest of the international aviation community. The airline community, with the support of the aircraft manufacturing community, passenger representatives (with a few, a very few, vociferous dissidents) and governments, have brought about the "dawn" of unlimited liability. But, what will the "day" bring, as some governments, notably the USA, seek to prolong the "dawn", other governments are reluctant to face the "new day" and still others are considering returning to the "evening" of the day before, although a brighter one than the one left behind?

1. The Dawn of Unlimited Liability

The "dawn of unlimited liability" may properly be attributed to the development and the coming into effect of the IATA Intercarrier Agreements of 1995 and 1996. These are the IATA Intercarrier Agreement on Passenger Liability (the IIA), adopted unanimously by IATA carriers at the IATA Annual General Meeting in Kuala Lumpur on October 31, 1995, and the IATA Agreement on Measures to Implement the IATA Intercarrier Agreement (the MIA), opened for signature in May, 1996. As of 11 May 1997, there are 87 signatories to the IIA and 53 signatories to the MIA. Also, as of 11 May 1997, 33 carriers had taken steps to implement the MIA, including the airlines of Japan which effectively did so in 1992.

A. The Substantive Principles of the IIA

The IIA simply is an agreement among IATA carriers:

1. "to take action" to waive the Warsaw Convention limitation on recoverable compensatory damages in cases arising under Article 17 of the Convention; and

2. to waive available Article 20(1) Convention defenses up to a specified monetary amount, reserving all available defenses above the specified amount.

There are other undertakings in the IIA, but they are not of significance to this paper.

B. The Substantive Principles of the MIA

The MIA was drawn up in an effort to provide some uniformity in the manner in which signatory carriers would implement the substantive principles of the IIA. The MIA obligates signatory carriers to incorporate *in their conditions of carriage and tariffs, where necessary,* the following provisions:

1. [Carrier] shall not invoke the limitation of liability in Article 22(1) of the Convention as to any claim for recoverable compensatory damages arising under Article 17 of the Convention;

2. [Carrier] shall not avail itself of any defense under Article 20(1) of the Convention with respect to that portion of such claim which does not exceed 100.000 SDRs.

C. The ATA Intercarrier Agreement

The Air Transport Association of America (ATA) formulated a separate implementing intercarrier agreement. The ATA Intercarrier Agreement (IPA), formally entitled "Provisions Impelementing the IATA Intercarrier Agreement to be Included in Conditions of Carriage and Tariffs", tracks the IATA MIA, with a provision for the law of the domicile as an integral part thereof, i.e. not an option as in the case of the IATA MIA.

The US carrier members of the Air Transport Association (ATA), pursuant to the DOT Order 97-1-2 of 8 January 1997, have implemented the waiver of the Convention limitation of liability envisaged by the IATA Intercarrier Agreements by tariffs filed with the US DOT. The ATA member carrier tariffs incorporate the applicatino of the law of the domicile of the passenger to the determination of recoverable compensatory damages, at the option of the passenger, if acceptable to the court in which the case is filed. The ATA member carriers also have agreed to provide a form of advice to their passengers as to the new Warsaw regime, but the wording of the agreed advice is unintelligible and meaningless at best, at least if its purpose is to tell passengers that the Convention liability limits have been waived, that Article 20(1) defenses have been waived up to 100.000 SDRs of the damages claimed, and that the law of the passenger's domicile may be relied upon to assess recoverable compensatory damages.

2. The Evolution of the Dawn of Unlimited Liability

The emergence of the IATA IIA and MIA and the ATA IPA did not happen "overnight". In fact, the first IATA Airline Liability Conference (ALC), convened in 1995 to address the subject of airline liability, had as its stated objective the updating or replacement of the 1966 Montreal Agreement. The process leading to the dawn of unlimited liability actually had been initiated by the airlines of Japan some three years earlier. The following is the chronological evolution of this new dawn.

1992 — The airlines of Japan effectively took steps *together*, without prior antitrust discussion immunity, to waive the Convention limitaion of liability for passenger injury or death and to waive the Article 20(1) defenses up to 100.000 SDR. This action quickly came to be known as the Japanese Initiative.

1992 - 1993 — Although not required, DOT approval of the Japanese Initiative was sought by the airlines of Japan and, by three separate Orders of the DOT, the Japanese Initiative was approved as being in the public interest of the United States and thereby its citizens and passengers.

1993 — The Japanese Initiative did not find any supporters in the international community, primarily, if not solely, because certain interests in the United States continued to assure their international colleagues that the ratification of MAP3 and the enactment of the SCP legislation by the United States Congress was imminent, when clearly neither was going to happen. In September 1993, IATA requested the DOT to grant the IATA carriers antitrust discussion immunity to enable the IATA carriers to meet and discuss the updating of the 1966 Montreal Agreement.

1994 — While the IATA application was deliberately and purposefully left to languish at the DOT, the Clinton Administration formed a special White House Discussion Group to explore the possibility of finding a solution to the MAP3 impasse (remember, these creatures had their origins in 1971) acceptable to all "conflicting" interests, airlines, passengers, manufacturers and US government interests. During the meetings of this Group, from July 1994 through October 1994, the adoption of the Japanese Initiative was urged by representatives of passengers and manufacturers as the best solution on the horizon, but this solution to the impasse was rejected by the Air Transport Association (ATA) and the DOT as not representing any significant change in the Warsaw Convention liability system, which causes protracted litigation with passengers, and as imposing liability on airlines under circumstances where airlines should not be liable, such as terrorist attacks, bombs and missiles. The Japanese Initiative also did not solve the DOT desire for a "fifth jurisdiction" and the application of US damage law to all claims involving US citizens or residents, the "law of the domicile" concept.

1995 — After the White House Discussion Group was disbanded in October 1994, having failed to reach any generally acceptable solution to resolve the MAP3/SCP impasse, the DOT, in February 1995, granted IATA the antitrust discussion immunity that had been requested in September 1993. The Airline Liability Conference (ALC) was quickly organized by IATA and convened in June 1995 in Washington, D.C. The ALC came together to discuss the updating of the 1966 Montreal Agreement but, as a result of the discussions at the ALC and subsequent ALC Working Group meetings in July in London and in Washington in August and September, the IIA evolved and was adopted unanimously at the IATA Annual General Meeting in Kuala Lumpur on October 31, 1995. The IIA committed signatory carriers "to take action" to waive the Convention limitation on carrier liability for passenger injury or death and to waive the Article 20(1) defenses up to a specified sum. The target date to implement the IIA was 1 November 1996.

1996 — As a result of further meeting of the IATA ALC Working Group, convened in Geneva in December 1995 and in Miami in January 1996, the MIA evolved as the agreed uniform means for IATA carriers to implement the substantive principles of the IIA. From January through July 1996, the DOT sent signals that the IIA/MIA package was not looked upon with complete favor because the agreements did not encompass the so-called "fifth jurisdiction" and the "law of the domicile" concepts. The DOT strongly desired the universal acceptance of these concepts so that US citizens and residents could always sue in the US and that US damage law always would apply in determining the types and levels of compensatory damages for US citizens and residents, regardless of where the action had to be brought under Article 28 of the Convention. The fact that neither concept could be imposed legally by any DOT action, or by any intercarrier agreement, was not acknowledged by the DOT, at least publicly. In July 1996 IATA filed the IIA and MIA with the DOT for formal approval. In October 1996, the DOT issued an Order to Show Cause why the IIA and MIA should not be approved temporarily, with numerous conditions attached, and coupled with a proposed program to find a way to resolve the perceived problems associated with the unattainable (without treaty amendment) concepts of the "fifth jurisdiction" and "law of the domicile". The Order to Show Cause proposals were severely criticized by IATA and other interested parties. As a result, the DOT in November 1996 issued a further Order (96-11-6) which approved the IIA without any conditions, but which conditioned approval of the MIA on "the law of the domicile" option in the MIA being made mandatory for transportation to, from or with a connection or stopping place in the USA. The approval of the IIA and the MIA in Order 96-11-6, was only temporary.

1997 — In December, 1996, IATA asked the DOT to reconsider the conditional approval of the MIA and, as a result, the DOT, in January 1997, issued Order 97-1-2 approving the IIA and MIA without conditions, but again only on a temporary basis until further Order of the DOT or 30 June 1998, whichever comes first. Order 97-1-2 effectively has approved, as the accepted means for IATA carriers to implement the 1995 IIA, the Japanese Initiative of 1992! In Order 97-1-2, the DOT reversed its November 1996 position and announced that it would accept for filing by IATA carriers and not reject tariffs implementing the IIA by adopting the obligatory provisions of the MIA, i.e., the waiver of the Convention limitation of liability and the waiver of Article 20(1) defenses up to 100.000

SDRs. In addition, the DOT announced in Order 97-1-2- that (1) IATA carriers filing tariffs implementing the IIA by adopting the obligatory provisions of the MIA would be exempted from all DOT regulations relating to the 1966 Montreal Agreement and (2) the MIA, as to those carriers, would replace the 1966 Montreal Agreement.

3. A Cloud on the Horizon of the New Dawn

Only a very small number of non-US carriers to date have taken steps to implement the waiver of the limit of liability in accordance with the IIA and the MIA. The major US carriers have implemented the IPA by tariffs filed with the US DOT. Of course, the airlines of Japan effectively implemented the MIA back in 1992 when they adopted the Japanese Initiative approach. Only approximately 10 non-US, non-Japanese airlines, have implemented, in one way or another, the MIA.

The most frequently asked question, on the dawn of this new era, is whether the waiver of the liability limitation by the ticketing or first carrier, is a waiver by all interline carriers who have not as yet implemented the MIA. This is but one of the commercial concerns arising in the early hours o the new day of unlimited liability.

Until there is universal uniformity on the implementation of the IIA by IATA carriers, there will be concerns as to the scope of the application of the waiver of the Convention limitation of carrier liability and Article 20(1) defenses by one carrier, where the transportation actually is performed by another carrier, which has not yet implemented the IIA. These concerns can be addressed in the conditions of carriage and in the commercial agreements of the involved carriers. The implementing conditions of carriage should provide expressly that the conditions apply to the carriage performed only by the carrier whose conditions apply to the carriage performed only by the carrier whose conditions of carriage they are.

Assume, for example, that carrier A has implemented the MIA by appropriate conditions of carriage but carrier B has not. In a *code-sharing operation*, the waiver of the Convention limitation of carrier liability and Article 20(1) defenses by carrier A would be applicable to all passengers on aircraft operated by carrier A, regardless of which carrier's ticket was involved. The waiver also would be applicable to carrier A ticketed passengers on aircraft operated by carrier B, where the carrier box in the carrier A tickets designates carrier A as the carrier for the flight sector actually performed by carrier B. The conditions of carriage of carrier B would apply to all other passengers on the aircraft actually operated by carrier B.

In *interline transportation*, only the conditions of carriage of the actual operator of the aircraft would be applicable to all passengers. Thus, in the example above, for aircraft actually operated by carrier A, the conditions of carriage of carrier A would apply to all passengers on the aircraft. For aircraft actually operated by carrier B, the conditions of carriage of carrier B would apply to all passengers on the aircraft, even those passengers traveling pursuant to carrier A tickets on the interline sector performed by carrier B.

The commercial agreements between carriers engaged in codesharing operations, or similar "joint operations", can and should allocate the relative shares of passenger liability as between the participating carriers. In the code- sharing example of carrier A and carrier B above, the code-sharing agreement could provide that carrier B will indemnify carrier A up to the limit of liability applicable to carrier B, but not beyond, except perhaps for an accident caused by the Article 25 wilful misconduct of carrier B, in which event carrier A could be fully indemnified by carrier B. The liablity insurers of both carrier A and carrier B should be made fully aware of the commercial arrangements, so that there can be no possibility of a gap in insurance coverage, regardless of the cause of the accident giving rise to the claims.

The concerns exemplified by the example of carrier A and carrier B discussed above will continue until the waiver envisaged by the IIA and the implementation envisaged by the MIA become universal among IATA carriers. However, these concerns are not insurmountable and can be addressed effectively in the interim by carefully worded conditions of carriage and the commercial agreements between carriers.

The interline and code-sharing problems that can arise in respect of the IATA Intercarrier Agreements are compounded by the law of the domicile option adopted by the ATA member carriers pursuant to the ATA IPA.

Until universality sets in, if ever, personalization of conditions of carriage and tarrifs, by stating that they apply only to carriage performed by the carrier whose conditions of carriage and tariffs they are, coupled with appropriate provisions apportioning liability in code-sharing agreements and similar "joint operation" arrangements, would appear to be the only means of confining the new Warsaw regime to transportation performed by the implementing carrier.

4. What will the Day Bring?

It is not too often that fovernment *reaction* to private initiative serves to brighten one's day. Hopefully, the *reaction* of governments to the private initiative of IATA will not serve to turn the clock back but rather will result in univeral (or virtually so) improvement of the Warsaw system, so that the 1992 light from the East which has served to illuminate the 1997 dawn throughout the world, will not be darkened by government measures presently being considered and already in force in the USA.

The Warsaw Convention system of liability must and should be preserved. Where modernization is desired, and there is very little modernization required, it should be accomplished by treaty amendment. That is precisely what the International Civil Aviation Organization (ICAO) set out to do in November 1995, spurred on by the adoption of the IIA by IATA in October 1995. In the interim, the Japanese Initiative, now embraced fully by the DOT, serves to resolve the most pressing problems of today associated with the 1929 Convention – the limitation of carrier liability for passenger injury or death and protracted litigation to overcome the limitation – without compromising or jeopardizing the sound uniform choice of law principles embodied in the Convention.

A. The Work of ICAO

My fellow panelist, Dr. Ludwig Weber, Director Legal Bureau, ICAO, will report the ongoing activity of ICAO in seeking to bring about modernization of the entire Warsaw system.

ICAO, spurred on by the achievements of IATA, is considering the adoption of a new instrument, representing the modernization of the Warsaw system and consolidation, in one instrument, of existing and effective agreements comprising the Warsaw System. The significant features under consideration, in the realm of passenger liability, include strict liability of the carrier to a stated amount (100.000 SDRs seems to be the benchmark), unlimited liability upon proof of fault (negligence seems to be the benchmark), the inclusion of the 1971 Guatemala City Protocol "fifth jurisdiction" and the incorporation of the 1961 Guadalajara Convention.

The objective of ICAO should be to amend the present Warsaw Convention, rather than to adopt an entirely new Convention, so as to preserve without question the validity of the vast body of legal precedent throughout the world interpreting the provisions of the Convention. The efforts of ICAO, if successful, should preserve the Convention for decades to come as the soundest international choice of law instrument ever devised.

B. The Work of the European Commission

My fellow panelist Frederik Sørensen of the European Commission, DG VII, will report in detail what is being done in the Commission with respect to European Union member carriers. It is hoped that whatever ultimately emerges from this government action will not serve to impede or recede the achievements of IATA in any respect. But I am not the one to suggest what the European Commission should or should not propose for its constituents.

C. The Work of the United States Government

The spokespersons for the United States government are determined to achieve these objectives, in the realm of international air transportation:

1. Strict liability.
2. No liability limitation.
3. The fifth jurisdiction.
4. The law of the domicile.

These objectives have not been achieved through the IATA process. However, the IATA Agreements and the ATA Agreement have been approved by the US DOT only provisionally until 30 June 1998 or further Order of the DOT, whichever is earlier.

The efforts of the US Government are now concentrated in the ICAO proceedings.

It is significant that desired objectives 1, 3 and 4 are not a part of US domestic law applicable to domestic and non-international transportation. Jurisdiction in US courts must still be based upon domestic law concepts and although the generally accepted rule is that the law of the domicile of the passenger applies in assesing recoverable compensatory damages, this is a court made rule and is not necessarily applied in every case. These has not been a meaningful limitation on recoverable compensatory damages in passenger injury or death cases in the USA for some 30 years.

Meanwhile, the US governement has entered the field of air crash disaster claims handling by virtue of the "Aviation Disaster Family Assistance Act of 1996", a Section of the Federal Aviation Reauthorization Act of 1996. The act directs that each US air carrier submit for approval "a plan for addressing the needs of the families of passengers involved in any aircraft accident involving an aircraft of the air carrier and resulting in a major loss of life". Now that is an interesting concept – "a major loss of life". One ponders – what would be a "minor loss of life"?

The Act is too convoluted and complex to summarize in a meaningful manner. Therefore, the complete Act is attached to this paper.

Several questions arise:

1. Who is going to pay for what the government has directed be done by air carriers?

2. The Act provides at the very end that nothing in the Act is to be construed "as limiting the actions that an air carrier may take...in providing assistance to the families of passengers involved in an aircraft accident". What then is the real practical objective of this Act? Is it merely more politics or does it have any purpose? Does the government even know what air carriers and their insurers do routinely to assist families of passengers involved in an aircraft accident?

This Act is the direct result of the clamoring of a very few, fueled by politicians and the media, in the aftermath of the tragic TWA 800 disaster of July 1996. Air carriers in the US, with the full support of their insurers, have been dealing with the aftermath of aviation disasters in an exemplary manner for decades. Of course, there have been some unfortunate mix-ups or foul ups, but these are the rare exception rather than the commonplace rule. Where will the government be if an air carrier does precisely what the 1996 "Family Assistance Act" says it must do and the families take exception? Certainly not standing behind or beside the air carrier or its insurers.

This is one area that the government should stay out of. There is no need for governement intervention. Law should not be enacted to alleviate problems that arise from exceptions to prevailing practice which has worked so well for so long for so many.

One wonders how many experienced airline personnel, insurance claims personnel, underwriters or aviation attorneys, on both sides of the bar, were consulted by the proponents of this Act or by the Congress before enactment? Would none be a hazardous guess?

Not to be outdone by the Legislative Branch (Congress) of the government of the US, the Executive Branch (State Department), spurred on by the same clamoring few, fashioned a Memorandum of Understanding (MOU in government lingo) to deal essentially with aviation disasters occuring outside of the United States and involving United States citizens. A copy of this MOU is attached. It is not known how many airlines have signed this MOU with the US State Department.

One wonders – how many incidents have occured in the part involving deficiencies in dealing with the matters covered by the MOU which the MOU will now eliminate? Who is going to pay for the added administrative costs imposed on the airlines by the MOU "Best Practices and Procedures"? How is the government handling of the matters included in the MOU going to improve by putting the responsibility for proper government function on the air carrier?

5. Conclusion

What will the day bring after the dawn of the new era of unlimited liability?

Eventually, one would hope, a universal system, built on the cornerstone of the Warsaw Convention of 1929, which takes into account the concerns of all regions of the world without compromising, to an unacceptable degree, the concerns of all regions. This may be asking for too much. But if the interests of the users of international air transport, the passengers, are given the top priority, as they should, and if the interests of governments for their domestic concerns are given due consideration, as they should, the light from the East that has illuminated the dawn of the era of unlimited liability should not flicker and die as the day goes on. In the meantime, and until the overriding interests of governments have been satisfied in acceptable amendments to the Warsaw System, the IATA Agreements should remain in place as the beacon for the future.

ANNEX I
U.S. AVIATION DISASTER FAMILY ASSISTANCE ACT OF 1996

TITLE VII-FAMILY ASSISTANCE
«49 USCA § 40101 NOTE»

SEC. 701. SHORT TITLE.
This title may be cited as the "Aviation Disaster Family Assistance Act of 1996".
SEC. 702. ASSISTANCE BY NATIONAL TRANSPORTATION SAFETY BOARD TO FAMILIES OF PASSENGERS INVOLVED IN AIRCRAFT ACCIDENTS.
(a) AUTHORITY TO PROVIDE ASSISTANCE.–

«49 USCA § 1136»

"(1) IN GENERAL.– Subchapter III of chapter II is amended by adding at the end the following:
§ 1136. Assistance to families of passengers involved in aircraft accidents

PL 104-264, 1996 HR 3539
(Publication page references are not available for this document.)

"(a) IN GENERAL.– As soon as practibable after being notified of an *aircraft accident within the United States* involving *an air carrier or foreign air carrier* and *resulting in a major loss of life*, the Chairman of the National Transportation Safety Board shall

"(1) designate and publicize the name and phone number of a director of family support services who shall be an employee of the Board and shall be respnosible for acting as a point of contact within the Federal Government for the families of passengers involved in the accident and a liaison between the air carrier or foreign air carrier and the families; and

"(2) designate an independent nonprofit organization, with experience in disasters and posttrauma communication with families, which shall have primary responsibility for coordinating the emotional care and support of the families of passengers involved in the accident.

"(b) RESPONSIBILITIES OF THE BOARD.– The Board shall have primary Federal responsibility for facilitating the recovery and identification of fatally–injured passengers involved in an accident described in subsection (a).

"(c) RESPONSIBILITIES OF DESIGNATED ORGANIZATION.– The organization designated for an accident under subsection (a)(2) shall have the following responsibilities with respect to the families of passengers involved in the accident:

"(1) To provide mental health and counseling services, in coordination with the disaster response team of the air carrier or foreign air carrier involved.

"(2) To take such actions as may be necessary to provide an environment in which the families may grieve in private.

"(3) To meet with the families who have traveled to the location of the accident, to contact the families unable to travel to such location, and to contact all affected families periodically thereafter until such time as the organization, in consultation with the director of family support services designated for the accident under subsection (a)(1), determines that further assistance is no longer needed.

"(4) To communicate with the families as to the roles of the organization, government agencies, and the air carrier or foreign air carrier involved with respect to the accident and the post-accident activities.

"(5) To arrange a suitable memorial service, in consultation with the families.

"(d) PASSENGER LISTS.–

"(1) REQUESTS FOR PASSENGER LISTS.–

"(A) REQUESTS BY DIRECTOR OF FAMILY SUPPORT SERVICES.– It shall be the responsibility of the director of family support services designated for an accident under subsection (a)(1) to request, as soon as practicable, from the air carrier or foreign air carrier involved in the accident a list, which is *based on the best available information at the time of the request*, of the names of the passengers that were aboard the aircraft involved in the accident.

(B) REQUESTS BY DESIGNATED ORGANIZATION.– The organization designated for an accident under subsection (a)(2) may request from the air carrier on foreign air carrier involved in the accident a list described in subparagraph (A).

"(2) USE OF INFORMATION.– The director of family support services and the organization may not release to any person information on a list obtained under paragraph (1) but may provide information on the list about a passenger to the family of the passenger to the extend that the director of family support services or the organization considers appropriate.

"(e) CONTINUING RESPONSIBILITIES OF THE BOARD.– In the course of its investigation of an accident described in subsection (a), the Board shall, to the maximum extent practicable, ensure that the families of passengers involved in the accident

"(1) are briefed, prior to any public briefing, about the accident, its causes, and any other findings from the investigation; and

"(2) are individually informed of and allowed to attend any public hearings and meetings of the Board about the accident.

"(f) USE OF AIR CARRIER RESOURCES.– To the extent practicable, the organization designated for an accident under subsection (a)(2) shall coordinate its activities with the air carrier or foreign air carrier involved in the accident *so that the resources of the carrier can be used to the greatest extent possible to carry out the organization's responsibilities under this section.*

"(g) PROHIBITED ACTIONS.–

"(1) ACTIONS TO IMPEDE THE BOARD.– No person (including a State or political subdivision) may impede the ability of the Board (including the director of family support services designated for an accident under subsection (a)(1)), or an organization designated for an accident under subsection (a)(2), to carry out its responsibilities under this section or the ability of the families of passengers involved in the accident to have contact with one another.

"(2) UNSOLICITED COMMUNICATIONS.– In the event of an accident involving an *air carrier* providing interstate or foreign air transportation, no unsolicited communication concerning a potential action for personal injury or wrongful death may be made by an attorney *or any potential party to the litigation* to an idnividual injured in the accident, or to a relative of an individual involved in the accident, *before the 30th day following the date of the accident.*

"(h) DEFINITIONS.– In this section, the following definitions apply:

"(1) AIRCRAFT ACCIDENT.– The term 'aircraft accident' means any aviation disaster regardless of its cause or suspected cause.

"(2) PASSENGER.– The term 'passenger' includes an employee of an air carrier aboard an aircraft".

«49 USCA Ch. 11»

(2) CONFORMING AMENDMENT.– The table of sections for such chapter is amended by inserting after the item relating to section 1135 the following:

"1136. Assistance to families of passengers involved in aircraft accidents".

«49 USCA § 1155»

(b) PENALTIES.– Section 1155(a)(1) of such title is amended.

(1) by striking "or 1134(b) or (f)(1)" and inserting ", section 1134(b), section 1134(f)(1), or section 1136(g)";

and

(2) by striking "either of" and inserting "any of".

SEC. 703. *AIR CARRIER PLANS* TO ADDRESS NEEDS OF FAMILIES OF PASSENGERS INVOLVED IN AIRCRAFT ACCIDENTS.

«49 USCA § 41113»

(a) IN GENERAL.– Chapter 411 is amended by adding at the end the following:

"§ 41113. Plans to address needs of families of passengers involved in aircraft accidents

"(a) SUBMISSION OF PLANS.– Not later than 6 months after the date of enactment of this section, *each air carrier holding a certificate of public convenience and necessity under section 41102 of this title shall submit* to the Secretary and the Chairman of the National Transportation Safety Board a *plan for addressing the needs* of the families of passengers involved in any aircraft accident involving an aircraft of the air carrier and resulting in a *major loss of life.*

"(b) CONTENTS OF PLANS.– *A plan to be submitted by an air carrier under subsection (a) shall include, at a minimum, the following:*

"(1) *A plan* for publicizing a reliable, toll-free telephone number, and for providing staff, to handle calls from the families of the passengers.

"(2) *A process* for notifying the families of the passengers, before providing any public notice of the names of the passengers, either by utilizing the services of the organization designated for the accident under section 1136(a)(2) of this title or the services of other suitably trained individuals.

"(3) *An assurance* that the notice described in paragraph (2) will be provided to the family of a passenger as soon as the air carrier *has verified that the passenger was aboard the aircraft* (whether or not the names of all of the passengers have been verified) and, to the extent practicable, *in person.*

"(4) *An assurance* that the air carrier will provide to the director of family support services designated for the accident under section 1136(a)(1) of this title, and to the organization designated for the accident under section 1136(a)(2) of this title, immediately upon request, a *list* (which is based on the best available information at the time of the request) *of the names of the passengers aboard the aircraft* (whether or not such names have been verified), and will periodically update the list.

"(5) *An assurance* that the family of each passenger will be consulted about the disposition of all remains and personal effects of the passenger within the control of the air carrier.

"(6) *An assurance* that if requested by the family of a passenger, any possession of the passenger within the control of the air carrier (regardless of its condition) will be returned to the family unless the possession is needed for the accident investigation or any criminal investigation.

"(7) *An assurance* that any *unclaimed possession of a passenger* within the control of the air carrier will be retained by the air carrier *for at least 18 months.*

"(8) *An assurance* that the *family of each passenger* will be consulted *about construction by the air carrier* of any *monument to the passengers,* including any inscription on the monument.

"(9) *An assurance* that the treatment of the families of nonrevenue passengers (and any other victim of the accident) will be the same as the treatment of the families of revenue passengers.

"(10) *An assurance* that the air carrier will work with any organization designated under section 1136(a)(2) of this title on an ongoing basis to ensure that families of passengers receive an appropriate level of services and assistance following each accident.

"(11) *An assurance* that the air carrier *will provide reasonable compensation* to any organization designated under section in 1136(a)(2) of this title for services provided by the organization.

"(12) *An assurance* that the air carrier will assist the family of a passenger in traveling to the location of the accident and provide for the physical care of the family while the family is staying at such location.

"(13) *An assurance that the air carrier will commit sufficient resources to carry out the plan.*

"(c) CERTIFICATE REQUIREMENT.– After the date that is 6 months after the date of the enactment of this section, the Secretary may not approve an application for a certificate of public convenience and necessity under section 41102 of this title unless the applicant has included as part of such application a plan that meets the requirements of subsection (b).

"(d) LIMITATION ON LIABILITY.– An air carrier shall not be liable for damages in any action brought in a Federal or State court arising out of the performance of the air carrier *in preparing or providing a passenger list pursuant to a plan submitted by the air carrier under subsection (b),* unless such liability was caused by conduct of the air carrier which was grossly negligent or which constituted intentional misconduct.

"(e) AIRCRAFT ACCIDENT AND PASSENGER DEFINED.– In this section, the terms 'aircraft accident' and 'passenger' have the meanings such terms have in section 1136 of this title".

«49 USCA Ch. 411»

(b) CONFORMING AMENDMENT.– The table of sections for such chapter is amended by adding at the end the following:
"4113. Plans to address needs of families of passengers involved in aircraft accidents".

«49 USCA § 4113 NOTE»

SEC. 704. ESTABLISHMENT OF TASK FORCE.
(a) ESTABLISHMENT.– The Secretary of Transportation, in cooperation with the National Transportation Safety Board, the Federal Emergency Management Agency, the American Red Cross, *air carriers, and families which have been involved in aircraft accidents* shall establish *a task force* consisting of representatives of such entities and families, *representatives of air carrier employees*, and representatives of such other entities as the Secretary considers appropriate.
(b) GUIDELINES AND RECOMMENDATIONS.– The task force established pursuant to subsection (a) shall develop.
(1) *guidelines to assist air carriers in responding to aircraft accidents*;
(2) *recommendations* on methods to ensure that attorneys and representatives of media organizations do not intrude on the privacy of families of passengers involved in an aircraft accident;
(3) *recommendations* on methods to ensure that the families of passengers involved in an aircraft accident who are not citizens of the United States receive appropriate assistance;
(4) *recommendations* on methods to ensure that State mental health licensing laws do not act to prevent out-of-state mental health workers from working at the site of an aircraft accident or other related sites;
(5) *recommendations* on the extent to which military experts and facilities can be used to aid in the identification of the remains of passengers involved in an aircraft accident; and
(6) *recommendations* on methods to improve the timeliness of the notification provided by air carriers to the families of passengers involved in an aircraft accident, including.
(A) *an analysis* of the steps that air carriers would have to take to ensure that an accurate list of passengers on board the aircraft would be available

within 1 hour of the accident and an analysis of such steps to ensure that such list would be available within 3 hours of the accident;

(B) *an analysis* of the *added costs to air carriers* and travel agents that would result if air carriers were required to take the steps described in subparagraph (A);

(C) *an analysis* of any *inconvenience to passengers*, including flight delays, that would result if air carriers were required to take the steps described in subparagraph (A); and

(D) *an analysis* of the implications for *personal privacy* that would result if air carriers were required to take the steps described in subparagraph (A).

(c) REPORT.– Not later than 1 year after the date of the enactment of this Act, the Secretary shall transmit to Congress a report containing *the model plan* and recommendations developed by the task force under subsection (b).

«49 USCA § 41113 NOTE»

SEC. 705. LIMITATION ON STATUTORY CONSTRUCTION.

Nothing in this title or any amendment made by this title may be construed as limiting the actions that an air carrier may take, or the obligations that an air carrier may have, in providing assistance to the families of passengers involved in an aircraft accident.

ANNEX II
MEMORANDUM OF UNDERSTANDING
REFLECTING BEST PRACTICES AND PROCEDURES

Recognizing the need for cooperation and mutual assistance following aviation disasters outside the United States involving United States citizens, and mindful of the provisions of the Aviation Security Improvement Act of 1990 (Public Law 101- 604); and with a view to addressing these important concerns, the signatory air carrier ("the Airline") and the United States Department of State ("the Department"), also hereinafter referred to as "a Party" or "the Parties,", will achieve the following:

1. Designation of Points of Contact

A. Within two weeks of when this Memorandum has been signed by the Parties, the Parties will exchange information concerning their *respective key personnel* within each entity who would have decision-making, policy, operational, and implementing roles *in the event of an aviation disaster outside of the United States.*

B. The information exchanged should include an initial point of contact office, available 24-hours a day, seven days a week, which would be in a position to alert key operational officers to an incident.

C. In addition to names and telephone numbers of key personnel, the Parties shall designate respective primary and alternate facsimile numbers available for the immediate receipt of important information.

D. Each Party will provide the other with any toll-free number(s) it intends to make available for use by next-of-kin in a crisis situation.

E. The Parties will exercise diligent efforts to continuously update, as necessary, the information specified in this segment.

2. Information Sharing

A. Upon learning of a *situation outside the United States* that has affected the health and safety of U.S. citizen passengers, the Party receiving such information will alert the other Party at the earliest opportunity to allow both *the Airline and the Department* to begin preliminary actions to meet their responsibilities. A Party should exercise its good judgment in deciding whether the matter warrants advising the other. *This provision creates no obligation to transmit information that has not been judged specific and credible.*

B. This alert should include the following information, if known:

(1) the air carrier and flight number;

(2) the flight's point of origin, destination, and any intermediate stops;

(3) the time, location, and nature of the incident; and

(4) the number of U.S. citizen passengers and any information on their condition.

C. The Department will advise any U.S. embassy or consulate affected, unless it is the source of the information.

3. Exchange of Liaison Officers

A. Within two hours of the initial notification of an aviation incident abroad, the Parties will confer regarding the feasibility and desirability of exchanging liaison officers between their respective crisis centers, in both the United States and at the site of the incident, to facilitate communications between them.

B. The advisability of such an exchange would depend upon the nature, duration, and severity of the aviation incident abroad.

C. In instances where the Parties agree that it is not necessary to physically locate liaison officers in each other's crisis centers, each nonetheless should assign one of its employees on-site in its crisis center to serve as liaison officer with the other.

D. Within thirty days after this Memorandum has been signed by both Parties, the Parties will advise each other of the names of the persons designated to serve in the role of liaison officer so that efforts can be made to provide these individuals with information and training to familiarize them with the internal procedures of the other Party's organization.

4. Duties of Liaison Officers

A. The general duties of the respective liaison officers are: (1) to apprise the Party to whom he/she is liaison of significant actions being taken by the Party whom he/she represents; (2) to keep the Party whom he/she represents informed of steps being traken by the Party to whom he/she is liaison; and (3) to ensure adequate prior consultation between both Parties regarding decisions which have the potential to affect both.

B. The liaison officer at all times should be provided sufficient information from the Party he/she represents to be able to brief key personnel of the Party to whom he/she is liaison.

C. The liaison officer should serve as the main conduit from whom and to whom all information is passed between the Parties.

D. When the Parties confer directly concerningn matters of mutual interest, the liaison officer should participate in, or at least be aware of, the content of those discussions.

E. The liaison officer should provide the Party to whom he/she is liaison with copies of all statements issued publicly by the Party whom he/she represents so that both Parties are familiar with information being provided to the media. When at all possible, such statements should be made available prior to their public dissemination.

F. The liaison officer should exchange information enabling both Parties to provide consistent and accurate updates to affected family memebers.

G. The liaison officer should provide the Party whom he/she represents with copies of summaries prepared by the Party to whom he/she is liaison describing the current state of affairs as it pertains to that Party's efforts to deal with the situation. The Department liaison officer will provide reports consistent with applicable security regulations governing classified material and laws and regulations on personal privacy.

H. The liaison officer immediately should establish procedures to identify and handle high priority calls, e.g., those received from persons apparently related to passengers on the flight in question.

I. The liaison officers should work wih the Parties' respective on-site representatives to promote effective consultations at the site on matters such as (1) coordinatnion with foreign officials; (2) the recovery and transport of remains; and (3) the handling of personal effects.

5. Cross-Training

A. Each Party will conduct sessions to familiarize the other with its *crisis management prodecures* and facilities, including simulation exercises to assess the practicality of the steps outlined above.

B. Each Party will make efforts to participate in each other's training exercises to gain an appreciation of the other Party's methods and procedures.

6. Passenger Manifests

A. Consistent with the purposes of Sec. 203 of the Aviation Security Improvement Act, the Parties will work for the exchange of timely and accurate passenger manifest information.

B. Accordingly, the Airline shall transmit to the Department the names of passengers and any additional information consistent with that outlined in Sec. 203 of the Aviation Security Improvement Act of 1990 to assist in identifying a point of contact for each passenger. *The Airline will provide an unverified manifest within three hours of the Airline being notified of an event.*

C. The Airline will update the information referred to above as it becomes available.

D. Each page of a manifest transmitted should bear the notation: "Manifest of (*Date/time*) – Subject to Refinement – Not for Public Dissemination".

E. The Department shall treat passenger manifest information it receives from the Airline *as privacy-protected under the relevant statutory* authority and not disclose such information by any method (written, oral, or electronic) unless such disclosure is authorized by law. Information provided to the Airline by the Department will be shared within the Airline on a need-to-know basis and will not be disclosed otherwise without Department approval.

F. Upon receipt of passenger manifests, if necessary, the Department will initiate an internal review of the passport record of the individuals listed to attempt to gather information identifying next-of-kin or other representatives. As stated in the Notice published in the Federal Register of August 2, 1995, such information can and will be made available to the Airline, upon request, to assist in identifying next-of-kin should this become necessary.

G. In consultation with the liaison officer of the Airline, the passenger manifest may be used to assist in identifying high priority incoming calls, i.e., those calls from persons who appear related to a passenger whose name is listed on the passenger manifest.

H. The Department will fulfill the responsibility assigned to it by Sec. 204 of the Aviation Security Improvement Act "to directly and promptly notify the families of victims of aviation disasters abroad concerning *citizens of the United States* directly affected by such a disaster, including timely written notice... notwithstanding notification by any other person". The Department will ensure that such notification occurs notwithstanding best efforts by the Airline to make prior notification.

7. General Provisions

A. Nothing in this Memorandum is intended to alter or supersede the provisions of any current or subsequent regulations implementing the provisions of the Aviation Security Improvement Act of 1990 (Public Law 101-604).

B. This memorandum may be amended by agreement of the Parties. It shall remain in force until terminated by 30 days written notice.

For the Airline: For the Department of State:

(Signature)   (Signature)
(Name)   (Name)
(Title)   (Title)
(Name of Airline)   (Date)
(Date)

Developments concerning the new ICAO draft convention on air carrier liability

by Ludwig Weber
Director of Legal Bureau, ICAO, Montreal

It is a great pleasure to be with you this morning and to speak about developments concerning ICAO's initiative to modernize the Warsaw System in promoting a new draft Convention on Air Carrier Liability. I wish to congratulate the organizer of this Conference, Dr. Nikolai Ehlers, for having chosen the right topic for this gathering at a very appropriate time, and for having attracted an impressive group of speakers. A discussion on liability in international air transportation could not be more timely; only 3 days ago, the ICAO Legal Committee concluded its 30th Session, having the subject of the modernization of the Warsaw System on top of its agenda.

1. Background

Efforts to modernize the Warsaw System have recently gained increased momentum throughout the international aviation community and have, particularly since ECAC's Recomendation of 1994, been the subject of widespread activities in various international fora. I therefore would like to briefly recap the events which led to the development of the new above-mentioned draft Convention and will then discuss the deliberations of the Legal Committee of ICAO.

2. Development of draft instrument

The starting point for the development of the new ICAO draft instrument was a decision of the 31st Session of the ICAO Assembly (19 September - 4 October 1995), which directed the ICAO Council to expedite the modernization of the "Warsaw System". Consequently, the Council decided in December 1995 to establish a Secretariat Study Group, which was mandated with the task of assisting the ICAO Legal Bureau in developing a framework for a modernized regime of air carrier liability. It was set up in January 1996, shortly after finalization of a socio-economic study on air carrier liability limits which ICAO carried out in co-operation with the International Air Transport Association (IATA) and which was to serve as an economic basis for the new initiative, in particular as regards liability limits. The membership of the Study Group was comprised of aviation law experts reflecting a broad geographical representation and various legal schools of thought. The Study Group produced a set of recommendations which were submitted to the ICAO Council during its 147 Session. These recommendations called, *inter alia,* for the development of a new international instrument in order to consolidate and modernize the "Warsaw System". This approach was considered to be of importance so as to prevent further fragmentation of the Warsaw Regime through a multiplicity of amending protocols, supplementary instruments and arrangements between air carriers. In line with these recomendations, which the ICAO Council approved, the Legal Bureau, assisted by the Study Group, was entrusted with the task of developing a first draft of a new instrument. During its second meeting, which took place in Montreal in June 1996, the Study Group adopted a first draft developed by the Legal Bureau which was presented to the Council in October 1996. Additionally, in order to prepare further action on this matter, the Chairman of the Legal Committee appointed in October 1996 a Rapporteur on the subject, who was mandated to review and revise the draft text and to report thereon to the 30th Session of the Legal Committee. The Report by the Rapporteur, Mr. Vijay Poonoosamy of Mauritius, comprises a detailed review of the text of the draft instrument and also contains suggestions as to crucial areas, such as the question of the determination of damages, matters related to the burden of proof and the interrelationship between the draft Convention and other parts of the Warsaw System as it presently stands.

3. The new draft instrument

The new draft instrument was developed along the main lines of the framework of the Warsaw Convention while modernizing the provisions on liability and liability limits, on documentation requirements, and on other important features. The aim in following the main lines of the Warsaw Convention was to preserve the benefits obtained from judicial precedents dealing with the interpretation of significant provisions of the

Warsaw Convention, and thus some degree of continuity. At the same time, the provisions of the draft text seek to adapt the legal regime governing air carrier liability to modern-day requirements while being responsive to increased concerns about effective protection of the air transport user. For example, concerning the international transportation of cargo, the draft fully incorporates Montreal Protocol No. 4. The intention behind this was to reduce the current multiplicity and complexity of Conventions, Protocols and Protocol Amendments of the Warsaw System. It is mainly for this reason that the Study Group favoured the adoption of one comprehensive legal instrument whose acceptability to States will hopefully be enhanced by the integration of legal elements previously accepted by a large number of States (e.g. the Guadalajara Convention), and by the inclusion of provisions which adequately reflect the operational reality and experience.

4. Salient features of the draft instrument

The following shall provide an outline of the most significant elements of the draft instrument and the reasons for their incorporation in the original draft:

a. The draft instrument introduces a *two-tier liability system in* case of accidental death or injury or passengers:

i. in the first tier, a regime of strict liability applies with a liability limit of 100,000 SDR

ii. in the second tier, above the ceiling mentioned above, a regime of fault-based liability applies without numerical limits of liability. Since negligence is sufficient to trigger air carrier liability in the second tier, protracted litigation on the issue of "wilful misconduct" becomes obsolete.

At present, the draft instrument still contains square brackets on the question as to who shall bear the burden of proof for negligence or fault with respect to the second tier. As a matter of comparison, both the IATA Inter-Carrier Agreement and the EU Commission have proposed solutions in favour of the passenger, i.e. the Warsaw-type presumption of fault of the air carrier has been retained for the second tier. The discussions in the Legal Committee on this point have favoured this approach also without, however, coming to a final decision. The text which the Legal Committee has approved, leaves certain alternatives in square brackets regarding the option of States to determine the burden of proof when ratifying. A three-tier system was also considered, with the burden of proof on the carrier in the second tier, and on the passenger in the third tier. Some more work will be required on this point before the Diplomatic Conference convenes. In both tiers, however, only compensatory damages are recoverable and must be proven by the claimant. The defense of contributory negligence remains available for the carrier in both tiers. The draft text does not provide for an express rule on what types of compensatory damages are recoverable. However, the proposed draft preamble makes reference to the concept of restitution.

b. *Documentary provisions* are brought in line with modern-day requirements in order to facilitate the smooth flow of passengers, baggage and cargo. The draft text not only fully incorporates the provisions of Montreal Protocol No.4 on the cargo side, but also accommodates computerized ticketing for passengers and baggage. The interest of the passenger is fully taken into account since, under the draft text a paper ticket is no longer a requirement under the Convention, and the passenger can decide whether or not he needs a full printout of the ticket and baggage identification tag providing him with all relevant information concerning the contract of carriage. The rules for the passenger ticket and the baggage tag have been combined into one provision, thus acknowledging operational requirements stemming from aspects related to aviation security and immigration procedures. The notice requirement has been modified since the notice no longer needs to be provided in, or in conjunction with, the ticket.

c. Under the new draft instrument, an *additional (fifth) jurisdiction* may be available to the air transport user in qualified narrow circumstances, in particular requiring the carrier's commercial and/or operational presence in the jurisdiction concerned. The draft text contains wording for the inclusion of an additional jurisdiction available only upon the fulfilment of restrictive conditions requiring the carrier's commercial and/or operational presence in the passenger's home State. This approach reflects the idea that if an air carrier is offering services to and from a particular foreign country and sells tickets there and has established its own ticket offices and a commercial presence then the carrier must accept to be taken to court in this jurisdiction. In the case of an accident, the carrier should in this case also assume the consequences of its operational activity, including being sued in the passenger's home jurisdiction, irrespective of the location of the accident.

This matter was one of the most controversial issues in the discussions of the Legal Committee. A number of specific questions still need further consideration by the Diplomatic Conference, such as whether the carrier must have operations and a commercial office in the passenger's home State, or whether operations would be sufficient.

d. The draft instrument provides for the option of both parties to elect *arbitration* as an alternative means for the settlement of disputes. It also allows air carriers to offer higher limits on the basis of a *special contract.* It is envisaged to incorporate an update mechanism *(escalator clause)* into the new draft instrument in order to counterbalance the effects of inflation on the respective limits for baggage and cargo and the ceiling of passenger liability in the first tier.

5. Consideration of draft convention in the legal committee

The Legal Committee also extensively discussed the provisions of the Guadalajara Convention, which have been incorporated as Chapter V of the new instrument as to their need of alignment with such practices as code-sharing. While most provisions were retained without change, a modification was made to the rule concerning special agreements between the Contracting Carrier and the passenger. Such agreements may in the future also affect the actual carrier.

6. The management of aviation disaster "new segment"

Let me briefly draw your attention to another important aspect relating to the settlement of claims following an international aviation disaster. Besides our common endeavour to create a legal framework under which just and equitable compensation can be sought, we should not lose sight of the human aspects which are encountered in the aftermath of an accident. Tragedies such as the shooting down of KAL 007, the Lockerbie case and the recent TWA 800 explosion, for example, have increased our awareness that money alone cannot alleviate grief. Much to the credit of the work of Victims' Organizations, initiatives have been taken up in order to facilitate and improve co-operation and mutual assistance in reaction to aviation disasters. In October 1996, the U.S. Congress passed the *AVIATION DISASTER FAMILY ASSISTANCE ACT* of 1996, the first Act of its kind [published in this volume as Annex I to the paper by George N. Tompkins, Jr.]. It is designed to promote effective and more appropriate tools for aiding families of aircraft accident victims in the immediate aftermath of an aviation disaster and to coordinate the response to major accidents occurring in the United States. I believe that this is an important and worthwhile initiative; air carriers involved in a major crash are usually simply overwhelmed by the organizational and administrative burdens associated with coping with such major incidents. Matters related to the disposition of remains and personal effects of the victim, to ensuring timely notification of families of passengers involved, giving victims' families psychological assistance, the issue of timely identification of victims, cooperation with the accident investigation teams, with police investigations, as well as, on top of all these, matters relating to interaction with the public media simply cannot be appropriately handled by ad-hoc solutions. Air carriers neither have the expertise nor the necessary resources to be able to handle these matters adequately on an ad-hoc basis. The above-mentioned act designates a federal agency –in this case, the National Transportation Safety Board– to act as a focal point and liaison between the air carrier involved and the families in all matters related to the incident. The legislation is aimed to provide a co-ordinated crisis management system. Related to these efforts, the United States Department of Transport is currently also proceeding with a rule-making to require U.S. air carriers to collect basic information from passengers travelling on flight segments to or from the United States which would include, for example, the passenger's full name, passport number as well as the name of an emergency contact. It is my understanding that foreign air carriers would be required to collect this information as well from U.S. citizens. It remains to be seen if and how the colletion of such data may best be implemented; effective communication between the air carrier, travel agencies, as well as CRS-systems ensuring the transmission of these additional data by way of an enlarged passenger name record(PNR), would have to be established.

To conclude this matter, despite some practical problems in the implementation, I believe that the international aviation community, at large, has a common responsibility and a common interest to be prepared in responding adequately to the needs of the victims of disasters, over and above and beyond the pure issue of compensation. ICAO will therefore launch an initiative towards a system-wide approach in relation to this subject by developing guidance material on this subject for Contracting States, for use as appropriate.

7. Conclusion

As can be seen from the above, ICAO's efforts for a comprehensive modernization of the Warsaw System is well under way. The discussion of this subject in the Legal Committee has shown that States are willing to pursue the work on the draft Convention expeditiously. Subject to the comments which may be received from States during the mandatory comment period ending October 1997, it is envisaged that a Diplomatic

Conference be convened for the adoption of the draft Convention as soon as appropriate, and hopefully in the course of 1998. In addition, ICAO will assist Contracting States to ensure that the devastating effects of aviation disasters will be met with adequate responses in the field of crisis management and will further examine the means of promoting an appropriate approach concerning this matter on a system-wide basis.

Council regulation and claims handling in The Netherlands

by Angelike M. Van der Vliet
De Brauw Blackstone Westbroek, The Hague

There have been several initiatives to improve the level of protection of passengers involved in air accidents.

- Japanes airlines for example agreed in 1992 to abolish the liability ceilings of the Warsaw Convention and apply a system of strict liability for claims up to a certain amount.
- Another example is the 1995 Kuala Lumpur Inter-carrier Agreement on Passenger Liability initiated by IATA with the same provisions; an agreement on a voluntary basis for which initiative IATA is trying hard to get worldwide support.

Meanwhile, the European Commission has prepared its own proposal for uniform rules regarding air carriers' liability. The proposed Council Regulation was presented in February 1996 and covered – in short – four major issues:

1. the abolition of liability limits for death, wounding or any other bodily injury;
2. strict liability of the air carrier for damages up to a maximum of ECU 100.000 (which means: abolition of the 'due care defences');
3. mandatory advance payments in case of death or injury with far reaching obligations for the aircarriers.
   The advance payment (in case of death 50.000 ECU and in case of injury up to 50.000 ECU) has to be made within 10 days after the accident has occurred and can be offset against the sum of a final settlement. But the advance payment is not returnable under any circumstances;
4. the victim or his/her heirs may inititate legal proceedings in the EU

Member State where they are domiciled or permanently resident, even if such jurisdiction is not available to them under the Warsaw Convention (Article 28).

Last year, the European Parliament suggested some changes to the Commission's proposal, after which the Commission presented an amended proposal in January 1997.

Just three weeks ago (21.4.97) the Common Position of the Council was published.

The Regulation adopted by the Council differs from both proposals of the Commission and covers the next major issues:

1. abolition of liability limits for death or injury of passengers;
2. abolition of the due care defences for any damages up to a maximum of 100.000 SDR (equivalent to 120.000 ECU); this means "strict liability" for the air carrier (up to that amount) *unless* the carrier proves that the damage was caused, or contributed to, by the negligence of the passenger; in that case the carrier may be exonerated (wholly or partly) from its liability;
3. mandatory advance payments "as may be required to meet immediate economic needs on a basis proportional to the hardship suffered".

This advance payment has to be made within 15 days after identifying the natural person entitled to compensation.

In case of death the advance payment has to be at least 15.000 SDR per passenger.

The advance payment may be offset against the sum of a final settlement, but is not returnable except in case of:

a. contributory negligence of the passenger; or if
b. the person who received the advance payment was not entitled to compensation.

The Council deleted the 5th jurisdiction rule proposed by the Commission on the grounds that the other four jurisdictions provided by the Warsaw Convention were sufficient.

You might expect that the Regulation would have been improved since the first proposal of the Commission, but unfortunately new questions have arisen. Without being complete, due to my limited time, I would like to make some critical observations:

1. First of all the rules regarding advance payments

Although the Council changed those rules in favour of the air carriers, they are still unrealistic and could lead to serious problems resulting from the time pressure caused by the 15 days deadline and the fact that the advance payment is in principle not returnable.

With regard to the mandatory advance payment of 15.000 SDR in case of death it has to be said that in certain jurisdictions within the European Union (for instance The Netherlands) recoverable damages are limited to loss of support and funeral expenses.

When we talk about loss of support according to Dutch law, there can be several persons entitled to compensation in case of death. Not just the spouse and children of the deceased, but also other relatives or life companion(s) who were supported by the deceased.

An advance payment in case of death of (at least) 15.000 SDR per passenger. What does this mean: "*per* passenger"?

Imagine the next case. The deceased apparently supported four persons:

    a) his spouse (they were not living together anymore, but not divorced either),

    b) his 19-year old son (who went to college),

    c) his old mother,

    d) his mistress (with whom the deceased was living together and their little baby of 6 months). Each of them files a claim.

Does the air carrier have to pay the 15.000 SDR to the first person to come? Or has this amount to be shared between all of them? Or can they claim an advance payment of 15.000 SDR each?

Who knows? Practical problems can be expected, that is certain!

I do not think air carriers should be obliged to reward an advance payment claim on behalf of every person who just *seems* to be entitled to compensation for loss of support. The question whether this person has a justified claim depends after all on the fact whether he or she has an own income or not (earnings, life insurance, social security benefits etc.). It is most unlikely that an air carrier will be able to determine this within a deadline of 15 days.

One should not forget that in practice it will take months for persons entitled to compensation for loss of support, to file a properly documented claim.

Moreover, in lots of cases Dutch law states that there will be no recoverable loss of support at all, because people are well insured (for example through the employer of the deceased) and because of the existence of a comprehensive social security system. In such a case a claim with respect to the funeral expenses remains but even these expenses would normally be less than 15.000 SDR.

So what will happen? The air carrier has to make the advance payment in accordance with the Council Regulation. After a while he finds out he compensated the wrong person or he paid too much in accordance with the applicable law.

The person who was not entitled to compensation at all has to return the advance payment, so provides the regulation, but it is common knowledge that this will be almost impossible; this money will almost certainly be unrecoverable. And the person who actually was entitled to compensation but received (because of the time pressure) too much, does not have to repay at all!

Why does the Regulation contain rules with respect to advance payments?

With the strict liability provision in the regulation, in most jursidictions, like The Netherlands, the victim will easily have the possibility to claim an advance anyway, provided that he did not cause the damage himself.

> (for example: in the case of a passenger falling out of his seat during a period of turbulence while he did not have his seatbelt fastened whereas he was told to do so).

In the Netherlands this advance payment action can be brought for interim injunction proceedings; in that case the plaintiff will have a decision of the judge within about 14 days.

The judge will sustain this (preliminary) claim when it is likely that the victim has an urgent interest in the advance payment (in the words of the regulation: if the payment is required to meet immediate economic needs) and when it is more than likely that the carrier will turn out to be liable to the victim in the end.

As said, this judgement will be preliminary: when it is eventually determined that there is no liability to the victim, the latter has to return the advance payment, although this will be, as I said before, not likely to be realized, unless of course the advance payment was made against security.

In general the premise is that the victim should receive compensation for the damage he actually suffered. No more and no less. The abolition of the liability limits contributes to this premise. But there is no justification for the 15 days deadline and the rule that the mandatory advance payment is in principle not returnable. Why should an airline passenger be in a better position than any other person involved in an accident?

2. Position of recourse takers

The rule of strict liability improves the passenger protection; there is no doubt about that and this is all in accordance with the social views of today. But I wonder how far the Council has thought about the consequences for the recourse takers.

When the Dutch legislator introduced some new strict liablities (for example with respect to defective movables) in the Civil Code (which came into force in 1992) he provided that subrogated insurance companies and social security organisations with a legal right to take recourse, could not benefit from these strict liabilities (for reasons of limiting extra claims). What happens with the strict liability of air carriers?

The Council Regulation defines "the person entitled to compensation" as a passenger or any person entitled to claim in respect of that passenger, in accordance with applicable law.

According to this definition, recourse takers are, at least according to Dutch civil law, (legal) persons entitled to compensation, which implicates that they can benefit from the strict liability of the regulation.

Whereas the rule of strict liability will open the floodgates to waves of unwarranted claims anyway, it will also lead to an increase in recourse actions.

3. Bodily and mental injury

To provide more uniform rules in matters of air carriers' liability is what this regulation aims at.

However, the rules of the regulation just relate to death, wounding and any other bodily injury. Unfortunately, the Council did not provide a rule regarding damages relating to mental injury, whereas it is generally known that the implementation of the Warsaw Convention differs from state to state.

The Dutch Civil Code for example provides compensation for (material) damages as a result of bodily injury and/or mental injury. It is debatable whether in the case of purely mental injury the victim is entitled to emotional (immaterial) damages. Literally the Civil Code does not provide this, but opinions about this matter differ.

(Even more debatable is, although this is not within the scope of this subject, the question whether a third party has a right to compensation for mental suffering as a result of the death or injury of the victim. The Dutch legal system does not provide this either, but there is a test case on this subject pending, so a decision of the Supreme Court of The Netherlands can be expected within the not too distant future).

It would have been a good idea if the Council had taken the opportunity to try to provide for the mental injury matter as well.

Altogether the present Council Regulation seems to be a hasty piece of work and negative implications (for the air carriers) can be expected. Let us hope that the damage will remain limited and that the European Parliament will propose a revision as soon as possible.

The EU Council Common Position on Air Carrier Liability

PRACTICAL IMPLEMENTATION ISSUES

by Marc Frisque

General Manager, Legal & Social Affairs,
Association of European Airlines, Brussels

I should like to address some practical implementation issues arising from the Common Position adopted by the EU Council on 24 February 1997 with regard to the proposed Regulation on Air Carrier Liability. As we are now reaching the final stages of the community regulatory process of adoption, perhaps this seminar provides one of the last opportunities to focus on practical implementation issues which may still deserve further thinking and even review before a final decision is made.

From the European airlines' perspective, there is a major concern with the provision dealing with mandatory advance payments to be made by the carrier and serious difficulties in meeting the requirement to provide a summary of the regulation main features in a ticket document, the so-called notice issue.

"Prompt advance payments can considerably assist the injured passengers or natural persons entitled to compensation in meeting the immediate costs following an air accident". This is how the "whereas" clause no. 12 in the proposed regulation is formulated. Surely no-one would disagree with this statement of general principle.

The issue at stake, however, is that we need more than such a statement of general principle. And the question is relevant because there is a well-known best practice of the industry in the handling of claims. Airlines and their insurers have developed procedures, although generally unwritten, to cover every possible eventuality in order to provide immediate financial and other assistance to passenger victims of aircraft accidents. It is indeed in the mutual interest of an airline and its passengers that claims are handled with speed, sympathy and efficiency.

By nature, flexibility is required in the best interests of the passengers as the circumstances of individual passengers and their close relatives vary considerably from case to case. Assistance can take many forms and should not only be seen from a financial perspective. Also, there are local traditions and religious customs and possibly the availability of aid from national social security schemes or private insurances which have to be taken into account when handling claims.

The International Chamber of Commerce commented that "victims are not an homogeneous group with similar needs and priorities" and also argued that rigid and binding rules would be undesirable.

You also, Mr. Chairman [Harold Caplan], in a Lloyds Aviation Law publication, have expressed the view that "there is a tradition of relevant experience to accommodate all foreseeable post accident circumstances without the burden of a rigid obligation to make cash advances".

Still the Common Position includes in its article 5 such an obligation. It reads: "The air carrier *shall* without delay, and in any event not later than 15 days after the identity of the natural person entitled to compensation has been established, make such advance payments as may be required to meet immediate economic needs on a basis proportional to the hardship suffered". A second paragraph specifies that such an advance payment shall not be less than the equivalent in ECUs of 15.000 SDRs per passenger in the event of death.

The concept of advance payments was initially developed by the European Civil Aviation Conference in a recommendation on air carrier liability dated June 1994. It has been subsequently introduced by the European Commission in its regulation on air carrier liability at a time when the IATA inter-carrier agreements were being developed by the industry and where it was known that these agreements would not address the issue of advance payments.

Do we have similar requirements by law in the countries of the European Union? In France, since 1991, a system of lump sum payment exists, by means of a unilateral commitment of the Association of French Aviation insurers upon the supervision of the Ministry of Transport. The lump sum in case of death is, however, half of the amount included in the Community regulation.

In Germany and Austria, air carriers must by law insure their passengers against accidents with a minimum of 35.000 DM in case of death in Germany. The law in these countries does, however, not refer to an advance payment per se.

These are the very few exemples where the issue has been cosnidered in Member States. There are, however, no requirements by law for advance payments in case of an accident.

At international level, the issue was discussed in ICAO by a study group on the Warsaw system and it appears that the majority of the members were reluctant to endorse any proposal which would mandatorily require the air carrier to pay out a specified amount within a set period of time. It was believed that such a general obligation would not appropriately take into account the diversity of facts of each case and would not be responsive to the variety of local customs associated with the actual settlement of the claims. There were, however, suggestions that as flexibility should be maintained, a new instrument should contain some general principles recognising the existing practice.

The question is again raised: is there a need for more than general principles in the EU regulation? Or shall we phrase it differently: is there a proven need for imposing a rigid and unclear requirement? I propose this issue for debate. Member airlines of the Association of European Airlines have investigated the issue and have concluded that flexibility is definitely in the interests of passenger victims and, therefore, if anything is needed in this area of advance payments, it should take the form of a code of conduct based on the best practice of the industry.

Having argued about the principle, before leaving the subject, I should like to point out that the text of the Common Position on advance payments, although substantially improved as compared to the initial draft, raises at least two other points with regard to the implementation:

- no provision is made for dividing the 15.000 SDRs sum in the event that there are a number of claimants, or for dealing with a claimant who emerges after the full sum has been paid to others or for a case where the division of compensation between claimants in the final settlement differs from the division of the lump sum payment.
- 15.000 SDRs might still be high amount in some countries and in some circumstances. For instance, under UK law the airline's total liability in respect of the death of a child would be only

about $7000. The community regulation requires a minimum of $13.000 in case of death.

A Council regulation which creates private law rights and obligations must be clear, particularly where the intention is to improve and speed up settlement of claims. Given the differen legal systems in the European Union and the different circumstances in which a Warsaw convention claim may be made, it appears that it would be very difficult to achieve that necessary clarity in relation to advance lump sum payments.

The second issue has to do with passenger information and the obligation under Article 6, para. 2, for the carrier to include in the travel document, the ticket, a notice containing a summary of the requirements regarding Article 3 which is the new liability regime and Article 5 which deals with advance payments, "in plain and intelligible language". This causes practical implementation concerns for European Union airlines. It should be noted that it is not in their power to comply with this requirement for the IATA neutral ticket stock if this were to be opposed by non-EU airlines. Industry neutral ticket stock is universally standardised and used and the wording contained in such ticket must be agreed by all carriers, including any changes thereof. Such requirement would also prove to be incompatible with ticketless traveling.

Moreover, it should be acknowledged that adding a new notice in the ticket might confuse the passenger even more, clearly the opposite of what is intended, as he/she will be confronted with a plethora of notices, i.e. the Warsaw notice on liability limitation, the liability limitation notice for traffic to and from the United States and the EU liability regime notice. It is also doubtful whether the inclusion in a ticket document of information about, for example, advance payments in case of an accident, and air carrier' insurance obligation under Community law, would be very useful to the passenger. In any case, such information must be included in the carrier's conditions of carriage (para. 1) and must be available at carriers agencies' points of sale. This we believe offers enough additional guarantee for complete consumer information and I shall strongly advocate the removal of this requirement for practical purposes and in the interest of all parties concerned.

Aviation Liability
A Manufacturer's View

by Matthias Funk
Head of Legal Department
BMW Rolls- Royce GmbH, Munich

As a manufacturer of aero engines, BMW Rolls-Royce, a Germany based joint venture company, has gathered some experience over the recent years with mainly North American airframe manufacturers and airlines, and with sub-tier manufacturers, which support the following conclusions.

Traditionally, in the aviation industry the proper identification and handling of liability issues has always been one of the most central aspects of contracting with airlines and airframe manufacturers.

The case for this special attention in twofold:

— In the case of a product failure the potential of damage is particularly high, and

— The sales volume in terms of the quantity of units sold is rather low, compared to many other industries.

This results in a very high liability exposure per unit sold. Consequently, the engine manufacturers traditionally have put a special emphasis on structuring their liability in a manageable way.

One key aspect is that risks must not be assumed by the manufacturer which are not clearly attributable to his own sphere. Risks arising from the operation and use of the equipment must remain the responsibility of the respective operator. Otherwise, there would not be a reasonable economic basis for manufacturing aviation equipment.

In practice, what this means is that the manufacturer requires a definitive description of his liability in the contract with his customer and that liabilities over and above those stipulated are excluded.

The contract will define the manufacturer's obligations in case of a defect concerning his equipment and will usually contain very comprehensive warranties, covering years of operation and many flying hours, to the extent that the operator can rely on technical defects being removed as part of the manufacturer's responsibility.

Where as a result of a defect, however, an operator – and in particular an airline – incurs further costs, looses profit or in any other way suffers hardship, then there should not be a recourse against the manufacturer.

Such allocation of risks has been widely accepted over the years and forms part of today's economic basis of the aviation industry.

Where third party claims are involved, such as from aircraft passengers, the resulting exposure of the manufacturer requires insurance cover.

Recent Developments

A number of factors are having an influence on that balanced situation today:

The aviation industry has suffered from the general downturn in the market – particularly as was experienced by the airlines over the last couple of years. An intensified competition between the manufacturers selling to the airlines was the result. Also, the current recovery in air traffic comes at a time of fierce competition between airlines.

As a result today the airlines are increasingly cost conscious and more so then before, not only when it comes to acquiring equipment but also in terms of its operation.

Where manufacturers were seeking compensation for these effects through their aftermarket business, even this is under pressure now as it is increasingly usual nowadays that the manufacturer must "guarantee" certain key characteristics of his equipment's performance over extended periods of time, such as fuel consumption but also the cost per flying hour for spare parts or rework of the equipment. In what looks like a significant factor contributing to the cost of operation, the airline tends to seek the manufacturers commitment "not to exceed" levels, with a responsibility to contribute to the cost incurred in excess of the guaranteed amounts.

This development further emphasises and increases the need to avoid additional risks and costs elsewhere.

The current reformation of the airlines' liability under the Warsaw

Convention may be relevant in this regard. The move to greater liability is likely to have an impact on the manufacturers – and their insurers.

It may well be that a claimant will raise claims less often directly against the manufacturer, if he can now obtain a more comprehensive compensation from the airline; in any case the airline may well have an increased desire to seek recourse from the manufacturer.

In the given situation it will be increasingly important to structure the liability to the airline in a reasonable manner, and those manufacturers who have a direct contractual relationship with the airline / operator will get a better chance to do so. Lower tier suppliers will have to rely on limitations on liability to their customers but that would not remove their liability at law to the aircraft operator, thereby resulting in the need for insurance cover.

The IATA Agreements from the Aircraft Manufacturers' Perspective

by Ross Marland

Barrister of Maxwell, Marlan & Associates
(Loss Adjusters of London and Alderney C.I.),
Aviation Law Consultant to Clyde & Co
(An International Law Firm)

Introduction

I have been asked, at regrettably short notice, to consider the aircraft manufacturers' position following the IATA proposals for the unlimited liability of airlines to their passengers. I should point out that I am not a manufacturer, nor have I ever been employed by one, so what follows is not based on inside knowledge. However, lawyers have never been shy of talking with the confidence of the uninformed, and at least it means that I owe no allegiance to any particular manufacturer and can thus, I hope, put the industry's best case objectively. Since there has not been any testing of the new scheme yet in the Courts, my views must be speculative.

Warsaw Origins

To understand the manufacturers' position, I am afraid that it is necessary once again to go back to 1929, when the world's leading nations agreed in Warsaw to the system of uniform laws for international air transportation which is generally known as the Warsaw Convention. Many, indeed most, of the provisions are as valid today as they were then, which is a great compliment to the drafters of the Convention in what was a new industry. However compensation for the death of, or injury to, passengers has been the subject of sustained criticism, especially in the United States. The scheme was that the damages an airline would pay would be limited, but that the passenger need not prove any fault by the airline to recover those damages.

Unfortunately, due to a legal quirk, manufacturers were not given the same, or indeed any, protection, as the legal position both in the civil law and the common law countries was that they would be immune from suit – the so called contract fallacy. This changed, at least in the common law world, for those countries (including the United States) which still then followed English Law, just 3 years later. But this was too late for inclusion in the Convention.

Why attack the manufacturer?

As with any lawyer, the plaintiffs' lawyer's duty is to do his best for his clients. Faced with limited compensation available from airlines, unless he could prove that the airline was reckless or guilty of willful misconduct, he would naturally look to the aircraft manufacturer. Pausing there for a moment, against the airline he did not need to prove fault up to the limits of liability but from thereon he had a very onerous task in proving willful misconduct. Against the manufacturer he always had to prove fault, but then the damages were unlimited and, in appropriate cases, he could also recover punitive damages. He would therefore sue the manufacturer, and indeed anybody else that he could think of, as a matter of course, in the hope that something would emerge on discovery – the so called scatter gun theory of litigation.

Really Insurers Paying

Of course, when one talks of airlines' or manufacturers' liabilities, it is really the aviation insurers who are going to pay. The airlines or manufacturers might suffer some bad publicity, and where the airline makes a habit of crashing, or a certain type of aircraft keeps falling apart, there will doubtless be an adverse commercial reaction from the travelling public, but in most cases it is the insurer who pays the big dollars, and because the pool of aviation insurers is small, it tends to be the same people paying for all the defendants.

It is therefore in the interests of all the defendants and their insurers to co-operate in settling the legitimate passenger claims quickly, and only defending the more outrageous claims, rather than to fight each other where the only winners would be the lawyers, both plaintiff and defendant.

Origins of Funding Agreements

There was a halcyon period when Harold Caplan, the distinguished chairman of this morning's panel, and his colleague Alan Hunter, achieved a succession of co-operation deals between airlines and manufacturers and their respective insurers, to the ultimate benefit of all, including, of course, the passengers. Indeed there is one example where Harold negotiated such a cooperation agreement between a manufacturer and airline, not merely before a crash but actually before the aircraft purchase. However, the world moved on and this approach was forgotten, resulting in the debacle following the Turkish Airlines DC-10 crash in 1974.

Funding Agreements Now

After this debacle there has been a move back to post-accident funding agreements, although these are not without difficulty for airlines due to the very strong contractual language used in purchase contracts by manufacturers. The idea of a funding agreement, as opposed to a sharing agreement, is that you make a quick estimate of the rough proportions of exposure of each of the parties on the basis of what is known in the immediate aftermath of a crash. Each party then pays this proportion into a common pool to enable the claims to be dealt with. By the time that all the claims are finished it is assumed that the true cause of the accident will have been identified, and then by agreement, or arbitration, or even litigation, the parties make adjusting payments. Such agreements can be very simple and written on virtually one sheet of paper, but in some recent cases they have taken up to a year or more to negotiate and been about the same length as Tolstoi's War & Peace. But the need for such agreements depends on the fact that plaintiffs lawyers will attack the manufacturer.

The IATA Agreement and Art. 20

The IATA agreement has now removed the limit on damages but liability remains strict, or no fault, at least up to 100,000 SDRs. Beyond that, the airlines have a theoretical defence by which the carrier shall not be liable if he proves that he took all necessary measures to avoid the damage or that it was impossible for him to take such measures. This is a sort of force majeur or Act of God defence.

Read strictly it is meaningless because if all necessary measures to avoid the damage were taken it would not have happened. To make any sense it must be read as taking "reasonably" necessary measures. This defence has been little used in the past. Because of the low limits of liability it would probably cost more in lawyers fees to run the defence than to pay the limits, but in future I envisage airlines trying to use it far more to try to force plaintiffs lawyers to sue manufacturers or others, although I must say that many lawyers believe that it is virtually impossible to succeed with this defence.

Why Sue the Manufacturer post IATA

If these lawyers are correct it follows that in all but the freak cases such as a missile shoot down (although even there would not all necessary measures include infra red decoy dispensers, and other anti-missile defences?), the airlines have strict liability and unlimited damages. Now reconsider the plaintiffs attorney's position. He no longer has to sue the manufacturer as well as the airline to get his full compensation, so why go to the trouble and expense of proving fault against a manufacturer when he doesn't need to against the airline.

No Contribution and Volunteers

If the plaintiffs don't sue manufacturers, you would assume that the airline would - in appropriate cases - join the manufacturers into the litigation themselves as third parties. But of course in almost every case there is a contractual bar to this. Never mind, you say, the airlines can settle with the plaintiffs and then claim contribution or indemnity against the manufacturer. Not so. In many jurisdictions if one party settles a claim completely he cannot then claim contribution, even from co-defendants. But let's say that we are in a jurisdiction which does allow this. The obvious defence of the manufacturer is that there was a perfectly good Convention complete with liability limits which the airline voluntarily waived. If you pay as a volunteer you have failed to mitigate your losses and cannot then claim an indemnity for your generosity. The damages against the manufacturer would thus be capped at the Warsaw limit.

But let's forget all the legal theory, and go to the real commercial world for our game of poker. Imagine a carrier who has a large number of feeder type aircraft, say SAABs or ATRs, and one goes in when there is evidence of an airframe fault - icing problems or whatever. The carrier has consequential losses and his insurers have paid out a lot in compensatory damages and they think the volunteer and other arguments do not amount to a row of beans. Are they really going into court to argue that the equipment in which they carry millions of passengers is rubbish, because that is what they will have to do - I think not.

Can The Plaintiffs Sue Manufacturers?

Unfortunately for manufacturers, there is a possibility that the volunteer argument can be turned on its head by the plaintiffs. The theory is that the plaintiff settles with the airline, but as the excess over the Warsaw limit is voluntary they can treat it as a sort of ex gratia payment and still proceed against the manufacturer, thereby getting a double recovery.

The other variation of this argument is that the airline would settle as a result of a contractual cause of action, whereas the cause of action against the manufacturer would be in tort, or strict product liability. Under the Warsaw system the passenger can only sue in a limited number of jurisdictions, but it should also be recognised that if the trials were split in this way they could sue the manufacturer in another, possibly more advantageous, location. I will leave the extraordinary case of Pakistan International alone until the French Cour de Cassasion has finally decided it.

The future. Pre-Accident Agreements? No Insurance

Commercial considerations will doubtless come into play in the real world, and manufacturers still need to sell aircraft, and so it is entirely possible that purchase contracts in the future will have some form of risk sharing agreement between the manufacturer and airline, or a least an agreement that they will not take the volunteer defence. This would be a resurrection of Harold Caplan's initiatives of so many years ago in that it would be a pre-accident agreement. Many of you will be aware that Boeing is currently changing its aircraft purchase agreement, although at present there is no specific recognition of what might be called the IATA problem.

It will be interesting to see how an IATA case wil work out, especially if there is fairly cogent evidence of aircraft failure, but in the meantime an argument could be made out that manufacturers will not need to insure for product liabilities, at least once the IATA agreement is widely accepted.

Claims and Damages
Legal Obligations of a German Airport Operator

by Thomas Ross

Legal Counsel, Munich Airport (FMG)

The professional training of a German lawyer starts at the university with heaps of science and little practice; once he has passed his examination and starts his professional carreer, the situation gets reversed: heaps of practice, and only now and then a tiny rest of jurpsprudence. For a lawyer in an airport company, the situation is even worse – at least as regards the field of claims and damages. Slightly better are the prospects for scientific legal work concerning public law, especially when it comes down to applying for those innumerous approvals necessary under German public law for building a new airport or for expanding the facilities, not to forget the respective lawsuits. But this is not the subject of my speech, so let's come back to claims and damages and the legal obligations of a German airport operator in this respect.

I would like to start with a somewhat distant phenomenon: the fall of blue ice. I suppose that everybody here is familiar with blue ice – if not: if the sowage- tank-cap of an aircraft is leaking, in the cold upper atmosphere the trickling liquid freezes to a lump, which can break loose and fall to earth. Most cases of that kind are not noticed anyhow, because the blue ice lump lands in the fields or in the woods: but sometimes it smashes roofs or cars, or, in a still fortunate case, it only lies melting and stinking in a garden.

What has the airport operator to do with this? Nothing, because under the German air traffic act liability for damages caused by an aircraft lies with the aircraft operator exclusively. Nevertheless, just recently there have been attempts by authorities to urge airport operators to set up funds for indemnifying injured parties. Of course, German airport operators have opposed, up to now successfully: The precipitation of blue ice cannot be attributed to the airport operator, neither legally nor practically. I admit that this is not too comfortable a situation for the sufferer who seldom will be able to prove that a certain airline has caused the damge. Relief could only be afforded by the aeronautical authorities executing more strict technical checks.

Let's come to another phenomenon, closer to the airport and to the airport operator, both legally and practically. I am speaking of wingtip-vortices, air- turbulences which are produced by landing aircraft and which can damage roofs. At the ancient Munich airport near the city, we have been confronted with that phenomenon frequently, because the landing track went in rather low altitude over housing areas. I can remember an inn that had, so to speak, a subscription to beeing untiled or even unroofed at least twice a year. Legally, in this case too the liability lies with the aircraft operator. Though, there have been theories to hold the airport operator responsible for every damage or detriment around the airport – at least as a joint debtor together with the respective airline. I have always declined this eccentric and boundless theory – but actually, we have always – as all German airports do! – supported the houseowners and car-owners, extending one of our watchmen with a camera in order to establish the circumstances; we then commissioned craftsmen or mechanics to do the repairs, we payed them and then tried to find out the airline at fault and to recoupe from there – more or less successfully. I still remember a case, in which we debated a bill of some 500. – DM with an airline for months and months. By the way, the airline is not existing anymore. Eventually, I was fed up with their prevarications and delaying tactics and told them that now we would sue them. At that point, they pleaded guilty but confessed shortage of money: whether we would be contented with a round-trip-ticket Munich- Berlin? Of course we were...

At our new Munich airport, wingtip-vortices are no problem because the airport is situated in a less densely populated area, location and direction of runways have been chosen skilfully in order to avoid the overflying of housing areas. I told you the entire story to show the readiness of the airport operator to accomodate useless and exhausting disputes on the one hand and to keep peace with its neighbours, irrespective of the legal situation. I feel this is rights as long as it is the free decision of the airport operator.

But there are, as I already mentioned, attempts from outside to hold airport operators liable for events they are not in charge with. Increasingly, the impact comes from the European Commission. The latest example in this regard was the issue of denied-boarding compensations: There was EU-legislation in the pipeline to give the passenger an entitlement for compensation in case that the aircraft is overbooked and he is denied boarding. So far, so good – but in context with that, the commission considered to oblige airport operators – not the airlines! – to enlighten passengers on their new rights.

Airports Council International, our association, asked all member airports for comments; the comments were that there is no legal basis within the EC treaty for the Commission to impose such obligations upon airport operators. In most European countries, airports are run as economic entreprises. This status is often neglected by authorities, especially the EU Commission, which sometimes treats us as the housekeeper in a public piece of infrastructure financed by the taxpayers money – which is not the case.

In number and amount, the cases I mentioned are more or less marginal, though illustrative. The bulk of cases we encounter arises from our core business, which is accommodating passengers, providing concourses and lounges and carparks and, above all, groundhandling. As mentioned at the beginning of my speech, there are few legal problems – the legal basis of claims can be liability in tort or contractual responsibility, regardless whether the airport is the sufferer and claimant or the one who caused the damage and is called upon for compensation. As an attempt to amuse you and thus to attract your attention, I would like to show you a transparency of the approval document of the ancient Munich airport of 1938. As you see from this deed, it is plain and short and it contains a provision that the airport operator has to take insurances for liability, amounting to 200.000. – German Marks for personal injury and 20.000. – Marks for material damages. What cheap and modest times! By the way: The old airport was operated by us until 16 May 1992, when we moved to our newbuilt airport: the old one was dismantled and, being property of the city of Munich, became the site for building the new Munich fair.

The approvals for the new airport, I have not brought with me, because they are volumes of several hundred pages, with an entire library of explanatory materials and expert opinions behind. Our interest in this seminar is restricted on the provisions taken for liability: The condition runs to take insurance for liability amounting to 80 million German Marks. Actually, we have taken insurance about 750 million. To reduce the insurance premium, we have accepted an own share in the risk of 2.000. – Marks per case. The cases are ranking from grave over considerable to minor and even ridiculous. Often enough, claimants tend to hold us responsible for things we have nothing to do with, such as misleading flight information given by airlines, denied boarding, cars towed away by the police from no-parking areas, damages allegedly done by authorities during the baggage-check, and so on. Of course we decline but try to show the claimants the way to find their real partner. Even the frequent case of baggage being damaged or diverted to the wrong destination is, in first instance, a matter between the airline and its passengers, a case of contractual liability, and just in second instance the question arises wether the airline has recourse to the airport operator. The recourse-situation gives one of the rare legal problems: Our handling contracts with airlines contain the condition that the airport in view of claims of the airlines enjoys the liability-restrictions of the Warsaw Convention; on the other hand, the EU-council has adopted its common opinion concerning an intended council regulation on the liability of carriers arising from accidents. The common opinon was published in the official journal Nr. C 123 of 21 April 1997, and it stands to reason that it could have repercussions on the contractual relation between airline and airport.

To come back to the range of cases: After our experience at the new airport, it goes from 20. – DM for a grease-stained pair of trousers up to 2 millions for an aircraft wing damaged by collision with a bus – not to speak of the bus itsself. Claims from our side for damages caused by airlines or service providers went from some hundred odd for a broken window up to more than 500.000 for our de-icing gantry when an aircraft tried to pass through it in summer and crashed into the spraying beam. Again: All those cases could be settled without lawsuits, simply by establishing the circumstances and then getting into negotiations, including the insurer. By the way: The airport operators security brigade, 135 men belonging to my legal department, plays an important role in that game, because they are called to every accident or damage detected and do the fact-finding, including taking photographs, drawing sketches and making a first interview with parties involved, thus preserving evidence for the following proceedings.

Lawsuits arising from damages are rare; some actions resulted from building the new airport and were lodged by building companies: the biggest such action amounted to 45 million German marks and was served to us by a collection and delivery service, because the statement of claim consisted in some 70 volumes piled up on a palett. But again I am leaving my subject – just so much about that lawsuit, it ended with a compromise.

To end this speech, a short outlook into future:

Airport operators are trying hard to reduce the number of damages – and only the number can be influenced, not the dimension: by training, by motivation, by supervision; Munich airport's groundhandling departement has recently undergone the quality certification process succesfully; the extent of the single damage, when it has happened despite all endeavours, lies in God's hand!

At the same time, the EU has legislated on the so-called opening of the groundhandling market, an initiative which could end up with bringing new service providers to the apron with goals and objectives different from the airport operators. I am curious whether the same obligations to hold insurance as have been imposed on us will be imposed on these new competitors, not to speak of taking insurances exceeding the minimum requirements, as we did; in any case, we will have to monitor the proceedings thoroughly. I urge you to join us in this, in the interest of safety and of customers' satisfaction.

Airline Liability
An Insurer's View

by Wolf Müller-Rostin
Delvag Luftfahrtversicherungs-AG,
Cologne

Under the leadership of its General Counsel Lorne Clark, IATA and its member airlines have worked out the new IATA Intercarrier Agreement. After decades of seemingly endless discussions concerning increases of the limits of air carriers' liability, the new Agreement was declared effective by IATA on Valentine's Day 1997.

A Valentine's present for the airlines and their passengers? Maybe for the passengers, but definitely not for the airlines.

Under the Warsaw Convention, air carriers operating internationally enjoyed the benefit of liability limits that were inadequately low and thus an embarrassment to the aviation industry. A liability limit of USD 10,000 or USD 20,000 cannot be considered adequate in any country. But a limit of –let's say– USD 300.000 might very well be considered sufficient compensation in many less developed countries, not only in case of injury but also in case of death.

The discussions about what limit is adequate to protect the passenger have been going on for decades. Liability limits are not the only criterion for passenger protection, however. Most of these discussions in the past have failed to address the other key issue: the degree of additional material protection afforded the passenger by social insurance systems and the relative priority of passengers' rights of compensation and the social insurance carriers' rights of recourse. How crucial liability limits are in a given case is dependent on the regulations laid down in domestic law governing this interrelationship between passengers' rights of compensation on the one hand and insurers' rights of recourse on the other hand. It is thus no wonder that the pressure for the recent change of the liability limits originated in the United States, where the standard of living is high but the social insurance system is rather underdeveloped. The right to claim compensation from the actual or alleged wrongdoer, be he a manufacturer or a transportation carrier, has a much higher priority in a country where care must be taken to avoid falling through the holes in the social insurance safety net.

The "good old" liability system of the Warsaw Convention – which admittedly had one serious problem: inadequately low limits – has been replaced by a system of American-made rules of liability and evidence: no limits of liability and no proof of exculpation, at least up to SDR 100.000. In consequence this does not amount to an adaptation of the Warsaw Convention to today's environment, it amounts to the burial of the Warsaw system with repercussions that will be felt worldwide.

Since the Warsaw Convention has been adopted by virtually all nations, the consequences of its liability regime and any changes to that liability regime affect carriers at both ends of the economic scale: carriers operating in countries with extremely high standards of living and carriers operating in countries with low or even extremely low standards of living. If one of the objectives of the new Intercarrier Agreement, namely restoration of a uniform liability scheme, is to be achieved, then even those carriers operating at the lower end of the economic scale are bound to accept a liability regime that is of no benefit to the majority of their passengers and thus of no benefit to the carriers themselves.

The new regime consists of two elements: the element of strict liability up to SDR 100.000 and the other element of unlimited liability for presumed fault. Knowing how difficult it is for a carrier to rebut the presumption of fault, it can be said that the new regime creates for the first time absolute liability in real terms. The economic consequences of a liability regime without any limits are mainly insurance consequences. It is thus not surprising that one – I would call it conservative – estimate, voiced by the aviation insurance industry in March, was that the new regime would generate extra claims costs for insurers of about USD 300 million annually. The airlines are fortunate, but their insurers are less fortunate: There is presently overcapacity in the aviation insurance market, which means that premiums have been falling for the last couple of years. Present quotations of insurance premiums, reflecting the new liability regime, cannot be taken as indications of a long-term trend. What is actually needed in order to enable insurers to pass the *real* costs of the Intercarrier Agreement on to the airlines is experience: a proven case of uncapped limits inflating liability awards. Of course, we all do not want that to happen, but we all know that ultimately it is going to happen. Such an accident would quickly be followed by a hardening of the presently soft market conditions. It will then be the airlines who will pick up the tab for some inevitably huge financial payouts.

One useful piece of information about the effects abolition of the limits could have on premiums is a study recently conducted by a group of key underwriters concerning *current* average passenger settlement amounts for death compared to possible *future* settlement amounts for death once the Intercarrier Agreement has received widespread acceptance.

	Present figure	Future figure/IIA IPA	
Canada	USD 350,000	USD 525,000	= + 50%
U.S.A.	USD 2,5 million	USD 2,5 million	
Japan	USD 1,0 million	USD 1,- million	
Korea	USD 1,0 million	USD 1,0 million	
Rest of Asia	USD 275,000	USD 420,00	= + 50%
Europe	USD 300,000	USD 750,000	= +150%
Rest of world	USD 200,000	USD 300,000	= + 50%

In my opinion, this study sends three messages:

1) An increase of the liability limit to an amount of USD 750,000 would have been sufficient to cover the majority of claims, except for those claims in the U.S.A., Japan and Korea.

2) For carriers who are registered in those three countries and draw the majority of their passengers from those three countries, liability awards will remain the same for the majority of their claims. Consequently, their insurance premiums will probably also remain pretty much the same. Coincidentally, these air carriers seem to be among those who have been pushing most vigorously for the introduction of the new Intercarrier Agreement.

3) For carriers from the rest of the world, liability awards will rise sharply – and so in all likelihood will their premiums. Of course liability insurance premiums for carriers in Europe, for instance, will not go up by a full 150 percent to match the expected rise in settlement awards. Insurers will have to precisely determine the regional mix of passengers of a given airline in order to set the appropriate new premium. Most airlines do not

keep statistics on the nationalities of their passengers, and determination of the regional mix can probably only be achieved on the basis of the tickets counted at each point of sale, assuming that a ticket sold in Frankfurt is a ticket bought by a German national – an assumption that of course is not always correct.

Small carriers will probably be affected most by the inevitable increase in insurance premiums. Furthermore, if a small regional carrier that still applied limits were to enter into a code sharing-agreement with a major carrier that did not apply any limits, the indemnity clause in the code-sharing agreement would most likely require the Regional acting as the operating carrier to indemnify in full the Major. The Regional's insurers would have to pay damages to a passenger with whom the Regional had never concluded a contract of carriage. So even if the Regional decided it could not afford the insurance costs for operating limitless systemwide, it would still be forced to take out additional insurance for code- sharing carriage. Particularly the smaller carriers will have to thoroughly review their contractual obligations under interline agreements, code-sharing agreements and maybe under successive carriage.

There are some more factors adversely affecting the insurance premiums: It is highly doubtful that there will be relief for the air carriers and their insurers in the form of less litigation. With the removal of the liability limitation, the focus of liability litigation will shift from circumventing liability limits to obtaining the best possible award: Proving willful misconduct or gross negligence was the name of the game in the past; maximizing quantum will be the name of the game in the future. For many claimants litigation also serves the purpose of fact finding. What caused the accident? Who is to blame for it? So for that reason, too, litigation will stay with us.

We have to keep in mind that the majority of personal injury claims are not caused by catastrophic events but by minor injuries on board an aircraft. So not just the payouts after catastrophic events will increase; the costs of litigating attritional losses will most likely rise substantially as well. Under the old system of liability, settlements of attritional loss claims could often be reached at very reasonable levels or, in the case of travel involving the United States, at a level in the vicinity of the Montreal Agreement level of USD 75,000. The risks, the costs and the uncertainties inherent in proving Art. 25 WC usually did not justify litigation on attritional losses. This might change, however, because under the new system the preferable settlement to be reached by plaintiffs will be SDR 100,000.

Even worse: with a system of presumptive liability for unlimited damages in place, plaintiffs now have every incentive to litigate their cases in the hope of even exceeding the SDR 100,000 limit. The expectation voiced by the Working Groups which put the Intercarrier Agreement together, namely that litigation costs would be saved by waiving the liability limits, could prove to be a short- lived expectation.

The possibility of one interesting scenario was recently mentioned by Tom Whalen from the Washington law firm of Condon & Forsyth in a paper presented at a conference of the International Association of Defense Counsel: In the past, the plaintiffs' bar has developed many imaginative and innovative theories as to why the Warsaw Convention should not apply to a particular case in order to avoid the application of the liability limits set forth in the Convention. For the reason of being protected by the liability limits, airline defense counsels have vigorously sought to establish that the Convention applied to every possible case involving "international transportation" and that a plaintiff was precluded from invoking a state common law remedy providing for unlimited liability.

Under the new regime there could be a dramatic reversal of these traditional legal positions. Because the Intercarrier Agreement lifts all liability limits but retains the presumption of fault of the carrier, plaintiff's counsel will argue for broad application of the Convention while defense counsel will try to narrow its application, at least as long as punitive damages are not of any concern. Interesting litigation of how restrictive or broad the term "accident" is to be read will be one of the results of the new Intercarrier Agreement. Somebody will have to pick up the tab for that litigation, too.

I am afraid that for carriers there is also only little relief in sight through arbitration. As a matter of contract, arbitration has to be agreed upon by the air carrier and the passenger. It is hardly conceivable that any claimant with his residence in the United States or with jurisdiction in the United States and advised by an American attorney would ever choose to have his case decided by an arbitration panel instead of by an American jury.

Third parties such as ATC, airport operators or aircraft manufacturers will be even less inclined than they are now to share in the costs of an accident once all the responsibility has been channeled through the air carrier. The Intercarrier Agreement will provide third parties with effective immunity from suit. The air carrier will have to pay full compensation to the passenger but will most likely be unable to take recourse against any third party because of disclaimer clauses in their mutual contracts. Aircraft manufacturers in particular have perfected the art of formulating warranties and disclaimer clauses in the purchase agreements that preclude any possible recovery by the air carrier from the manufacturer. The loss of a potential co-liable party will also have a negative effect on air carrier's liability insurance premiums.

If the new agreement is not to the benefit of the air carrier, is it at least to the benefit of the passengers?

Maybe, but definitely not for the full amount. The primary beneficiaries will be the social insurance carriers, which under a system of limited liability would have to bear the major share of the passengers' damages. This is at least true in many European countries with well-developed social security systems. It might not be true in the United States. Under a system of unlimited liability, the social insurance carrier can indemnify itself against the air carrier by way of recourse for any and all payments made to the passenger. So in countries where there is a fully functioning social security system in place, it is the insurance carriers that will benefit most from the new Agreement. Was that really the intention behind the abolition of liability limits?

Overall, the IATA Intercarrier Agreement does not seem to be a good solution for a great number of carriers. They will be burdened with higher insurance premiums for insurance coverage that in many cases exceeds their need for adequate protection of their passengers. In all likelihood, the amount of litigation will not decrease; its focus will simply shift from circumventing the limits to maximizing quantum. The main beneficiaries of the new liability system will be social insurance carriers, who will be able to take recourse action against the air carriers for every cent paid out to the passengers, even though these insurance carriers had already collected insurance premiums from the passenger over all the years preceding the accident.

There is no doubt that the liability system of the Warsaw Convention was in dire need of reform. But why did the balance of the Warsaw system between presumed liability on the one hand and limited liability on the other hand have to be distorted to the detriment of the air carriers? Applying a limit, albeit on a much higher level, would have restored the old balance between passengers and carriers. Passengers and carriers come from countries with very different economic strenghts and standards of living. So giving passengers with high standards of living the option of obtaining additional insurance protection by paying a surcharge directly to the carrier would have resulted in a system creating a balance within the groups of passengers and carriers. The Intercarrier Agreement, however, favors those passengers at the upper end of the economic scale, at the expense of those passengers at the lower end of the scale.

Putting a limit on carrier's liability but at the same time giving the passenger an option to obtain additional insurance, if required, by paying a surcharge would not have put the passenger in any disadvantageous position. After all, there is the legal principle of freedom of contract. Any person is free to enter into a contract with another on the basis that his liability in damages is limited or even excluded when he is in breach of contract. Exclusion and limitation clauses are a common feature of commercial contracts and contracts of carriage are no exception. It is against that background, rather than a desire to provide remedies to enable *all* losses to be compensated, that the Convention must be judged. It was not designed to provide remedies against the carrier to enable *all* losses to be compensated. Rather, it was designed to define those situations in which compensation was to be available. It set out the limits of liability and the conditions under which claims to establish that liability were to be made. A balance was struck in the interests of certainty and uniformity. That balance has been severely distorted by the Intercarrier Agreement.

Limitation of liablity is inherent in all transportation law. The Intercarrier Agreement is only an interim measure until the Warsaw Convention is completely overhauled. Should such a deviation from the present system not have been left to an intergovernmental conference under auspices of ICAO?

IIA, MIA, IPA, EU Regulation, Warsaw limits, Hague limits, Montreal limits, limits of SDR 250,000 to be introduced by carriers from the Gulf area – the fabric of the most important element of the Warsaw Convention, namely its liability regime, looks like a piece of patchwork. The solution to avoiding this patchwork might sound outdated, but it is simple and easy to implement: A substantial increase in the liability limits plus the option for the passenger of obtaining additional insurance cover by paying a surcharge directly to the carrier if the passenger feels only a higher limit or no limit would cover him sufficiently.

But now this solution has been lost forever. Many do not regret this, but I do.

Airline Liability
An Insurer's View

by Wolfgang Schatz
Deutscher Luftpool, Munich

May I just take up my colleague's last remark:

If Dr. Müller-Rostin regrets that due to the Intercarrier Agreement better solutions are lost – then there are already two of us in this Club!

But I am afraid we have to accept that the Intercarrier Agreement is now reality and airlines as well as the insurance industry have to get along with this fact.

There is not enough time to comment on each point Dr. Müller- Rostin has raised in his presentation. Just allow me a few remarks on some practical questions and problems that we have to solve right now.

Let us stay a little bit longer with the Intercarrier Agreement:

Lorne Clark informed us this morning that almost 90 Airlines have now signed the Umbrella Agreement and maybe every day a few more will. But how do they implement it?

*

Remember, there are 2 option in the Implementation Agreement:
1. The "law of the domicile" provision and
2. the possibility of preserving the waiver of limits and defences (up to 100,000 SDR) solely for the passengers or their dependants and thus excluding the social security or similar bodies from these – voluntary – contractual benefits.

With these 2 options airlines still have
    a) a lot of influence on the final cost of a claim and
    b) they can at least try to make sure that the additional money that

will have to be spent really serves their interests and the needs of the passengers.

I think that every aviation insurer must have a vital interest in these questions and should stay in close contact with his clients to make sure that both sides have a common understanding of the implementation in detail – and of course its consequences. Because in the end the way this is done determines the exposure and should therefore have quite some bearing on the necessary surcharges.

*

There are many good reasons not to implement the law of the passenger's domicile. And I have the impression that most of the airlines feel the same way.

Just imagine the claims settlement in practice:

If all of you here in this conference room came to Munich on the same flight and had bad luck...

I would not want to be the insurer who has to settle all your claims according to your respective different national laws. But if I had to and if no agreement on this settlement could be achieved...

well then according to Article 28 of the Warsaw Convention, the place to go would be the District Court of Landshut, a small and cosy town some 20 miles away from here.

And now just imagine how this nice little court would have to apply American, British, French, Italian and maybe some other law in one big trial.

What an interesting experience! Also with regard to the possible time-frame of such a lawsuit!

*

Let us look at the other option in the Implementation Agreement: Dr. Müller-Rostin already pointed out that the primary beneficiaries of the Intercarrier Agreement would be the social insurance carriers.

And I am afraid he is absolutely right in this assessment. Airlines which adopt the Intercarrier Agreement and make no use of the second option I just mentioned might soon find out – at least here in Europe – that the ones who get the greatest portion of the additional money spent on an aircrash are not the passengers or their families, but in many cases the respective social security carriers.

What a waste of financial resources! Do airlines and their insurers really have to refinance – voluntarily – state-owned social insurance carriers?

Just to give you an idea of the financial dimensions we are talking about: A good example is the crash of an ATR 42 on a flight to Como in October 1987. This accident was – for various reasons – compensated on an "unlimited" basis. Among the victims were 29 Germans. The compensation to the German social security carriers amounted to over 10 million DM in addition to another 11 million DM for the families!

This accident took place 10 years ago. If you add the necessary increases for inflation (I think 30% for 10 years are not too much) then you have the financial level we are aiming at – even if other social security systems in Europe might be less expensive than the German one.

So my recommendation for every airline would be: Please make use of this option to allocate the waiver of limits and defences explicitly to your passengers and their families. I don't have to stress that this of course requires a very careful wording.

Unfortunately things became a little bit complicated by the latest position of the American Department of Transportation on this issue. Frankly I was quite surprised when I learned that the DOT would not accept this option with regard to American social agencies. I always thought that social security played no major role in the Americain claims handling practice. It now looks as if I am wrong in that respect – or was it just a political gesture, a kind of symbolic surrogate for the compromise on the law of the domicile issue? Perhaps our American colleagues here can give us some background information about the real motives behind the scene?

But anyway, I think it is still worthwhile to try to prevent – at least in Europe – that the Intercarrier Agreement becomes a fundraising exercise for state-owned insurers of social security! – Even if things might look quite different when the proposed European regulation comes into force.

But that is another story ...

Aviation Liability and the Impact of Change - View from a Distant Shore

by Philip Chrystal
Legal Counsel-Underwriter
Swiss Reinsurance Company, Zurich

In several of the world's major cities there are calendar clocks counting down the number of days before the year 2000. For the majority of the world's population this date seems to hold some special significance, although I think that for many their greatest concern is where and what they will be doing at midnight on the 31st of December 1999.

In Beijing another clock is ticking - counting down the number of days left before a somewhat different but equally momentous event; the reversion of Hong Kong from British to Chinese sovereignty. I think it is fair to say that the 30th of June assumes less importance for most in the world although at least 1.2 billion will definitely be commemorating the occasion. For the rest of the world it will still be a significant event all the same. I think its importance lies in the fact that Hong Kong is a symbol, a symbol of change in the late 20th century, reinforcing the point that the world is changing and changing at a rather remarkable pace.

Political implications of the reversion aside, if you simply look at Hong Kong in isolation from a purely economic and social stance and more particularly at the changes that have occurred in Hong Kong over the past 30 years you will be able to draw a very compelling example of how rapidly the world is changing.

I want to talk about change today, and I want to talk about the implications of change for the aviation insurance and reinsurance industries. I would also like to briefly touch upon the implications of that change for the legal profession. And I am going to use my symbol of change, Hong Kong, to illustrate the point. An odd choice you may think given the forum - a predominantly European gathering? Well, I could justify it on the basis that at least for another 49 days, Hong Kong remains a "European Union" colony. I would rather justify my choice, however, by moving immediately to my first point about "Change".

It sounds almost trite to talk about the shrinking world or the global village. Nevertheless, it's a fact, and two industries have in my opinion contributed to this reality. Firstly, the media. With 24 hour satellite access we probably know more about the events on the other side of the world, in Hong Kong, for example, than we do about our own local politics. The other industry which has greatly contributed to change is the one in which we all work in varying capacities - the aviation industry. We have literally shrunk the world by generating the means of unprecedented mobility.

Consider that when this photograph was taken of Hong Kong's Kai Tak Airport in 1966, 1.3 million passed through the terminal during the year. London's Heathrow by comparison processed 12 million passengers. Last year, Kai Tak handled 30 million passengers, Heathrow 56 million. It is also of interest to note that in terms of city pairs with the world's highest traffic volume, flights between Hong Kong and Taipei now rank third in the world in terms of international scheduled passenger traffic. This follows London-Paris and London-New York. In other words there has been an explosion of growth in terms of passenger numbers in the case of Hong Kong specifically and the world generally. More simply stated, "people are on the move".

Of course, aviation not only contributes to change, it also reflects change. In 1966, the Gross Domestic Product per capita in Hong Kong was approximately $ 570, Britain $1,966 and Germany $2,051. In 1994 Hong Kong's GDP per capita surpassed that of its "imperial benefactor" and last year the figure for Hong Kong was $27,130, Britain by comparison $20,900 and Germany $30,300. I hasten to add that my point in providing these figures is not to reinforce the Asian economic miracle. That is done on an almost daily basis by self-styled Asian experts although, of course, there is a point to be made which relates to our business concerning the realignment of the world's wealth.

Let us return to the photograph of Kai Tak in 1966 and now look at it from an aviation underwriter's perspective. The four aircraft in the picture are a mixture of piston, turbo props and first generation jet aircraft. For the aeroplane spotters in the audience more precisely, a Lockheed Electra L-118, DC-6B, Boeing 707 and for the real connoisseurs a Convair 880-22M. For the aviation underwriter they represented at the time hull exposures of collectively and approximately $13m - the Boeing 707-420 model, for example, with an an agreed value of $6.7 million, the Convair 880-22M, $4.2million.

In this photograph of Kai Tak taken last year there are ten aircraft featured, their agreed values ranging from $5 million for the L-1011 through to $170 million for the Boeing 747-400 models of which there are no less than four depicted. Accumulatively, that represents about $1.4 billion worth of hulls and exposure on the apron which is an increase of more than 10,000% and you will note that the aircraft are all located in a very concentrated and confined area.

There is another aspect of this change which should be of some interest to the legal profession. In 1966 the majority of the aircraft flying throughout the world were owned by their airline operators. In contrast, a recent survey of aircraft acquisition patterns by major airlines over the past ten years concluded that by 1996 only 16% of operators owned their entire fleet, 42% leased all their aircraft, while the fleets of the remaining 42% were mixed in the ratio of 60 owned - 40 leased. This means that there are now a substantially greater number of additional parties with legal interests in the aircraft who require financial protection from insurers for their assets and legal assistance on the odd occasion for recovery of the proceeds under the operators hull policy. Loss payee clauses under a primary insurance policy and reference to the contentious cut through clauses in a reinsurance slip introduce a new dimension to our business.

Returning to Kai Tak in 1966, what is interesting about this photograph is that the harbour is clearly visible from the observation deck. No longer. A massive land fill programme of the harbour adjacent to the single runway on the left was born of necessity in Hong Kong. Land has always been at a premium in Hong Kong and the recent sale of a private residence for $70 million and a new industrial estate land fill project which sold for in excess of $2 billion in March, ensures that Hong Kong can still maintain claim to possessing the world's most expensive real estate.

With the airport's infamous "kamikaze" east/west approach on Runway 13 over a densely populated area and some of the most expensive real estate in the world, the potential third party damage arising from a multiple engine failure on take off or a landing short of the threshold must rate as an underwriter's nightmare in terms of the third party damage. Third party damage being the great unknown in terms of assessing exposure because it is inherently random in nature. The El Al accident in Amsterdam demonstrates this point convincingly.

That rather tricky runway, incidentally, has earned Hong Kong the dubious distinction of being the site of the world's most expensive single hull loss to date; the overrun in November 1993 of an almost new Boeing 747-400 with a $145 million agreed value.

We have looked at the changes in the value of the equipment flying in and out of Hong Kong and we briefly speculated upon the potentially catastrophic consequences in terms of third party liability. Let us now complete the equation by examining those onboard the aircraft and their potential liability exposure.

Thirty years ago Hong Kong was described rather ungraciously as a "coolie colony". The numbers flying in and out of Hong Kong at the time were small - not surprising given a Gross Domestic Product per capita of $570. I assume, therefore that the majority of those who boarded the aircraft in my earlier photograph were either nonresidents or expatriates. This category of passengers was never inexpensive but the majority were still subject to the stringently enforced and widely accepted Warsaw Hague amended limits of $20,000. Fewer of course could have been travelling on the very recently introduced increased Montreal Agreement limits of $75,000 assuming they were travelling to, from or with an agreed stopping place in the United States. The average seating capacity was around 150 per jet aircraft. The airlines were probably buying around $300 to $500 million for combined passenger and third party legal liability. This translates as an estimated liability exposure per aircraft of $3 million. That permitted a very comfortable margin between the maximum possible loss and the policy limits of the time.

Gradually, of course, the seating capacity of aircraft has increased and Hong Kong probably has one of the highest concentrations of wide-body equipment in the world as this photograph attests to. Flights to and from Hong Kong also boast some of the world's highest load factors.

I have already referred to the marked increase in the GNP - and it is also worth mentioning that Hong Kong boasts the highest number of millionaires per square mile on earth. Curiously, another indicator of the growing economic affluence of those boarding flights in Hong Kong is represented by the turn over of airport duty free sales. Hong Kong ranks third in the world.

So what is the picture that is emerging of the demographics or profile of the passenger boarding a flight in Hong Kong in the 1990s? Well obviously they are far more affluent than they were 30 years ago and in terms of numbers and concentration per aircraft considerably greater. To complete the picture I mentioned the disproportionate number of expatriates and nonresidents boarding at Kai Tak in 1966, and they are still a factor to be reckoned with.

Assuming we say on a 747 with a capacity of 380 seats, 20% or 76 passengers are Japanese and 6% or 23 passengers are Americans. That gives a total "expensive or premium passenger" loading of around $130 million per aircraft. The rest of the passengers we would estimate bring the total exposure to nearly $ 200 million. - absent of any third party damage. At higher award averages for "non-premium" passengers, the exposure could easily exceed $ 300 million per aircraft - quite conceivable in the case of Hong Kong originating or terminating flights.

Compare that to the policy limits of $1 to $1.25 billion for combined passenger/third passenger coverage which airlines commonly purchase and while the margin is still comfortable, the gap appears to be narrowing. The impact of change should now become evident from the insurers' and their reinsurers' perspective.

Well, we have looked at the past and present but what does the future hold? As a reinsurer, we believe that the margin between policy limits and a maximum possible loss will continue to narrow with the possibility of a major catastrophe occurring - by which I mean a loss in excess of $ 1billion - becoming more probable.

The factors contributing to such a scenario include firstly, the most obvious growth - growth in air traffic. We have seen that there is a correlation between economic development and the growth in air transport. The Economist magazine in the editorial of their special publication predicting the course of 1997, noted that the world economy will grow at a rapid 4% this year. "More wealth", they predicted, "will be created in 1997 than in any previous year in history and since the rate of population growth is coming down, that new wealth will go further". So the economic environment is conducive to growth and so also is the political climate as the world begins to reassess the merits of bilateralism and strict regulatory control in favour of liberalisation of the airline industry.

Obviously, we will need new aircraft and possibly larger aircraft to satisfy the increased demand. That of course puts a greater strain on a currently over extended air traffic control infrastructure and on "capacity" exhausted airports throughout the world. In that respect, returning to my model of Hong Kong, there is good news. Arguably one of the world's most "demanding" airports will be replaced next year by one of the amazing feats of engineering this century.

The majority of the 35 million passengers who are expected to use this airport next year will bear little resemblance to those who boarded first generation jets in Kai Tak 32 years ago. Undoubtedly more affluent, more educated and more worldly, in the event of a loss I doubt they, their dependants or their legal representatives will consider settling for below their true economic value.

Recalling my first point about the influence of the media, I believe that the American preoccupation with legal redress will become a worldwide trend, if only because of the pervasiveness of American media. People are, as a result, becoming far less passive, and this coincides with a growing momentum for less government interference and more personal responsibility - the emergence of the so-called "Sovereign Self".

This leads me to another two factors which I believe will influence the liability trend. The first is a product of the realisation of the faltering and sometimes checkered performance of many governments "at running things". The IATA Intercarrier Agreements which were initiated by industry are testimony to the ineptitude of governments to address the issue of satisfying contemporary consumer expectations over the past three decades. As far as I am concerned, the agreements are a reality and as an underwriter, irrespective of my views on pricing aspects of their adoption, they determine the environment in which I now work.

The present assault on the welfare state will also have consequences on exposure and liability levels. In an environment where government overspend is more critically analysed by its constituents, there will be a greater number of state social security agencies endeavouring to recover from the carrier's insurers by way of subrogation. This is a concern that I know has been expressed on numerous occasions by the German and Dutch insurance community and it has been realised following a major aviation loss early last year.

How do we as reinsurers respond to the changes which I have outlined? As I mentioned, we see for the above reasons significantly heighten exposure over the next decade. At the same time, we see a continued concentration within our industry no different from that occurring in other industries. Accordingly, as a major reinsurer we are considering new approaches including what we describe as a "multi" policy concept. "Multi layered" for example, where we as reinsurers - highly capitalized financial institutions - concentrate on catastrophic losses, i.e. in excess of $1 billion. We are also further exploring the concept of "multi year" and "multi line" policies which would combine the non cumulative layers of catastrophe cover over multiple lines of business and over several years.

This is not an insurance forum so I will not go into any further details but we believe that change is inevitable and we must anticipate it. This brings me to my final point about the consequences of change in terms of our relationship with the legal profession.

Last week, I conducted two very interesting discussions with some of the most prominent legal professionals practising in the London market. We agreed on many things but one thing we agreed upon and it is actually stating the obvious - is the continued need for specialised legal expertise in this increasingly sophisticated market. The Intercarrier Agreement, has despite a rather valiant attempt, unfortunately, not provided the uniformity in terms of claims handling procedures that we were all seeking.

Issues such as addition of a fifth jurisdiction, or the interim measure whereby damages are quantified according to domicile or permanent residence, will all need to be resolved in the immediate future and they need the enlistment of competent and progressive legal practitioners, global in their outlook (as are their clients) who are prepared to respond to the world's changing commercial and social environment.

Speaking of a changing environment, in 49 days when the world's eyes are focused on the Royal yacht Britannia sailing out of Hong Kong harbour with a member of a European monarchy aboard together with his former colonial governor, spare a thought not only for the political implications of the event but consider also the dynamic economic powerhouse they leave behind them. And cast a glance during the internationally televised event at that remarkable and improbable airport protruding into the harbour and reflect upon change and the contribution of aviation to the creation of a 20th century miracle.

PROGRAMME

9:30-10:00	Registration, Coffee
10:00-10.15	Opening Address by *Professor P.D. Dagtoglou* (President of the European Air Law Association, London/Athens)
	Introduction: *Dr. P. Nikolai Ehlers* (Ehlers, Ehlers & Partner, Munich)
10:15-11:15	1st Panel: Governemnts/International Organisations
	Chairma: *E. Frietsch* (German Dep. of Justice, Bonn)
	Special Presentation: *Lorne S. Clark* (General Counsel and Corporate Secretary, IATA, Geneva)
	Panellists: *F. Sørensen*(Head of Air Transport Policy Unit, DG VII, European Commission, Brussels)
	G. Tompkins, Jr. (Tompkins, Harakas, Elsasser & Tompkins, New York)
	Dr. L. Weber (Director, Legal Bureau, ICAO, Montreal)
11:15-11:30	Discussion
11:30-11:45	Coffee break
11:45-12:45	2nd Panel: Carriers/Lawyers
	Chairman: *Harold Caplan* (London)
	Panellists: *N. Hughes* (Barlow, Lyde & Gilbert, London)
	B. Strömberg (Director, Customer Relations, SAS, Stockholm)
	A. van der Vliet (De Brauw Blackstone Westbroek, The Hague)
	M. Frisque (General Manager, Legal and Social Affairs, Association of European Airlines, Brussels)

12:45-13:00	Discussion
13:00-14:00	Lunch
14L00-14:30	Coffee
14:30-15:15	3rd Panel: Manufacturers/Airport Operators
	Chairman: *S. Matthews* (Lloyd's Claims Office, London)
	Panellists: *M. Funck* (Legal Counsel, BMW-RR, Munich)
	R. Marland (Barrister/London)
	T. Ross (Legal Counsel, Munich Airport)
15:15-15:30	Discussion
15:30-15:45	Tea
15:45-16:45	4th Panel: Insurers
	Chairman: *A.H. Bolton* (Chairman & Chief Executive, Bowring, London)
	Panellists: *Dr. W. Müller-Rostin* (Legal Counsel, DELVAG, Cologne)
	W. Schatz (Managing Director, Deutscher Luftpool, Munich)
	P. Chrystal (Legal Counsel, Swiss Re, Zurich)
	W. Ranieri (Vice President, USAIG, New York)
16:45-17:00	Discussion
17:00-18:15	Cocktail Reception

List of Participants

Delegates:	Job Title/function - Name of company/firm:	City, country:
Mrs. Bettina ADENAUER	Legal Counsel Deutsche Lufthansa	Frankfurt/Germany
Mr. John BALFOUR	Partner Frere Cholmeley Bischof	London/England
Mr. Armin BEIER-THOMAS	Senior Vice President Gebrüder Krose	Bremen/Germany
Dr. iur. Roland BENTELE	Rechtsanwalt SAirGroup/Swissair	Zurich/Switzerland
Dr. iur. Christian BENZ	Partner Benz & Partners, Law firm	Zurich/Switzerland
Mr. Anthony H. BOLTON**	Chairman & Chief Executive The Bowring Group Ltd.	London/England
Mr. Stefan BOVIN	Claims Manager Aviabel	Brussels/Belgium
Mr. Stanley BRATTMAN	Claims Manager, Syndicate 53 Crowe Syndicate Management Limited	London/England
Ms. Ina BROCK	Attorney at Law Attorneys Boesebeck Droste	Munich/Germany
Mr. Cor. A. BROUWER	Solicitor Van Traa Advocaten	Rotterdam/The Netherlands
Dr. Thomas BURCKHARDT	Attorney at Law/Partner Holliger Pfrommer & Partner	Basel/Switzerland
Mr. Hans Joachim BUES	Senior Director Munich Airport (FMG)	Munich/Germany
Mr. Harold CAPLAN**	Consultant	London/England
Mr. Philip CHRYSTAL*	Legal Counsel Swiss Re	Zurich/Switzerland
Mr. Lorne S. CLARK*	General Counsel and Corporate Secretary IATA	Geneva/Switzerland

Mr. Peter COX	Executive Director	London/England
	Nicholson Leslie Aviation Ltd.	
Mr. Scott CROSBY	Partner	Brussels/Belgium
	Kemmler Rapp Böhlke & Crosby	
Mr. Philip CROES	Lawyer	Antwerp/Belgium
Mr. John CRUSE	Director	London/England
	Nicholson Leslie Aviation Ltd.	
Prof. P.D. DAGTOGLOU* **	President of the European Air	London/England and
	Law Association	Athens/Greece
PD Dr. iur. Regula	Attorney at Law	Winterthur/Switzerland
DETTLING- OTT	Schiller Denzler Dubs	
Dr. med. Dr. iur. Alexander P.F.	Attorney at Law	Munich/Germany
ELHERS	Ehlers, Ehlers & Partner	
Dr. iur. P. Nikolai EHLERS*	Attorney at Law	Munich/Germany
	Ehlers, Ehlers & Partner	
Mr. Gunther ELBING	Attorney at Law	Munich/Germany
	Nörr, Stiefenhofer & Lutz	
Mr. Jean-Michel FOBE	Attorney at Law	Brussels/Belgium
	McGuire, Woods, Battle &	
	Boothe, L.L.P.	
Mr Soren FOGH	Attorney at Law	Copenhagen/Denmark
	Gorrissen, Federspiel,	
	Kierkegaard	
Mr. Edwin FRIETSCH**	Ministerialrat (head of section)	Bonn/Germany
	Federal Ministry of Justice	
Mr. Marc FRISQUE*	General Manager, Legal and	Brussels/Belgium
	Social Affairs	
	Association of European Airlines	
Mr. Mathias FUNCK*	Legal Counsel	Oberursel/Germany
	BMW- RR GmbH	
Mr. Markus GEISLER	Attorney at Law	Cologne/Germany
	Deringer, Tessin, Herrmann &	
	Sedemund	
Mr. Francisco GOÑI	Partner	Madrid/Spain
	Goñi & Co.	
Prof. Dr. Rodolfo A.	Lawyer	Madrid/Spain
GONZALEZ- LEBRERO	Goñi & Co.	
Mr. Andreas GRAN	Attorney at Law	Frankfurt/Germany
	Gran & Collegen	
Mr. Giuseppe GUERRERI	Lawyer	Rome/Italy
	Studio Legale Guerreri	
Mr. Craig J.M. HALBLÄNDER	Law Student	Southampton/England
	The University of Southampton	
Mr. Lars HOLO	Attorney at Law	Oslo/Norway
	Arntzen, Underland & Co.,	
	Law firm	
Mr. Nicholas HUGHES*	Partner	London/England
	Barlow Lyde & Gilbert	

Mr. Russ KANE	Consultant	Dublin/Ireland
	Parc	
Mr. H. Peter KEHRBERGER	Attorney at Law, Notary	Kronberg/Germany
	Kehrberger & Huesker	
Dr. Paul Michael KRÄMER	Sen. Research Associate	Cologne/Germany
	Institute of Air & Space Law	
Ms. Marijnen KREEK	General Counsel	Schiphol Airport/The Netherlands
	Transavia Airlines C.V.	
Mr. A. KROEGER	Dutch Aviation Pool	Amsterdam/The Netherlands
Mr. John LARKING	Senior Claims Manager	London/England
	ACE London Aviation Ltd.	
Mr. Henrik LIND	Lawyer	Copenhagen/Denmark
	Gorrissen Federspiel	
	Kierkegaard	
Mr. Amadeu LOPES SABINO	Legal Counsel	Brussels/Belgium
	Council of the European Union	
Mr. Ross MARLAND*	Consultant	London/England
	Clyde & Co.	
Mr. Peter MARN	Aerodrom Ljubljana	Ljubljana/Slovenia
Mr. Stephen MATTHEWS**	Manager & Adjuster, Aviation	London/England
	Group	
Mr. Dag MIDLING	Attorney at Law	Oslo/Norway
	Advokatene Midling, Nakken &	
	Christensen	
Mrs. Signe MOE	Head of Division	Oslo/Norway
	Ministry of Transport and	
	Communication	
Mr. Mohammed MOHAMMED	Legal Researcher	Safat/Kuwait
	Kuwait Airways Corporation	
Mr. Graeme MURRAY	Corporate Lawyer	Stansted Airport/England
	Air UK Ltd.	
Dr. Wolf MÜLLER-ROSTIN*	Legal Counsel	Cologne/Germany
	DELVAG	
Mr. Gàbor NEMESÁNSZKY	Head of Department	Budapest/Hungary
	Malev Hungarian Airlines	
Dr. Beate NETTELBECK	Legal Counsel	Grünwald/Germany
	Allgemeine Leasing GmbH & Co.	
Mr. Owen O'CONNELL	Partner	Dublin/Ireland
	William Fry, Solicitors	
Mr. Liam O'DALY	Legal Advisor	Dublin/Ireland
	Attorney General's Office	
Mr Ralf OELSSNER	Managing Director	Cologne/Germany
	Albatros Versicherungsdienste	
Mrs. Alda PATO	Advisor to the Board	Lisbon/Portugal
	TAP-AIR PORTUGAL	
Mr. Anders Carsten PEDERSEN	Director Legal Affairs	Copenhagen/Denmark
	Maersk Air	
Dr. Michael PRAGER	Attorney at Law	Vienna/Austria
Mr. William RANIERI*	U.S. Aviation Underwriters, Inc.	New York/U.S.A.

Mr. Bernhard RANKEL	Legal Counsel	Vienna- Airport/Austria
	Lauda Air Luftfahrt AG	
Mr. Thomas ROSBIGALLE	Manager, Legal	Munich/Germany
	ERC Frankona	
Mr. Thomas ROSS*	Legal Counsel	Munich/Germany
	Munich Airport (FMG)	
Ms. Jurate RUSTEIKAITE	Chief Legal Adviser	Vilnius/Lithuania
	Lithuanian Airlines	
Mr. Wolfgang SCHATZ*	Managing Director	Munich/Germany
	Deutscher Luftpool	
Mr. Florain C. SCHEIBECK	Trainee	Munich/Germany
	Ehlers, Ehlers & Partner	
Dr. Ronald SCHMID	General Counsel/Director Int'l	Oberursel/Germany
	Affairs	
	Aero Lloyd	
Mr. Jeremy SHEBSON	Solicitor	London/England
	Clyde & Co.	
Mr. Peter SMITH	Head of Branch - International	London/England
	Aviation Policy Division,	
	Department of Transport	
Mr. Frederik SØRENSEN*	Head, Air Transport Policy Unit,	Brussels/Belgium
	DG VII, European Commmission	
Dr. iur. Thomas SPAHNI	Attorney at Law	Zurich/Switzerland
	Stauffacher + Partner	
Mr. Giorgio STARC	Aviation & Space Claims Dep.	Trieste/Italy
	Assicurazioni Generali	
Mr. Hugh STEWART	Liability Consultant	Heathrow Airport/England
	Airclaims	
Mr. Bert STRÖMBERG*	Director, Customer Relations	Stockholm/Sweden
	SAS	
Mr. Algimantas STUCKA	Head of Legal Department	Vilnius/Lithuania
	Lithuanian Airlines	
Mr. George N. TOMPKINS, JR.*	Partner	White Plains, N.Y./U.S.A.
	Tompkins, Harakas, Elsasser &	
	Tompkins	
Mr. Dirk TURLEY	Underwriter	Munich/Germany
	ERC Frankona	
Mr. Walter UEBELHOER	Research Assistant	Cologne/Germany
	Zeitschrift für Luft.- u.	
	Weltraumrecht (ZLW)	
Ms. Angelike VAN DER VLIET*	Attorney at Law	The Hague/The Netherlands
	De Brauw Blackstone Westbroek	
Mr. Jean-Louis VAN DE WOUWER	Managing Director	Brussels/Belgium
	Homes International NV	
Mrs. Janneke VAN EXEL	Dutch Aviation Pool	Amsterdam/The Netherlands
Mrs. Anne VAN LANGENDONCK	Attorney at Law	Brussels/Belgium
	De Backer & Bastin	

Mr. Rui VERES	Aviation Counsel Cabinet of Transport Secretary of State	Lisbon/Portugal
Mr. Anne Margrethe VIKEN	Senior Executive Officer Norwegian Ministry of Transport and Communications	Oslo/Norway
Dr. Elmar VITT	Legal Counsel Nordic European Airlines Int. AB	Stockholm/Sweden Cologne, Bonn/Germany
Dr. Ludwig WEBER*	Director, Legal Bureau ICAO	Montreal/Canada
Mr. Geoffrey WHITE	General Manager Parc	Dublin/Ireland
Ms. Mia WOUTERS	Lawyer Lafili, Van Crombrugghe & Partners	Brussels/Belgium